Krzysztof Kubiak

Scapa Flow
Home of the
Royal Navy 1939–1945

STRATUS

Published in Poland in 2021
by STRATUS s.j.
Poland
e-mail: office@mmpbooks.biz
as
MMPBooks,
e-mail: rogerw@mmpbooks.biz
© 2021 MMPBooks.
http://www.mmpbooks.biz

ISBN
978-83-66549-03-6

Editor in chief
Roger Wallsgrove

Editorial Team
Bartłomiej Belcarz
Robert Pęczkowski
Artur Juszczak

Text and research
Krzysztof Kubiak

Translated by
Kazimierz Zygadło

Drawings and maps
Robert Panek

Drawings
Witold Koszela

Proofreading
Roger Wallsgrove

DTP
Stratus sp. j.

Printed by
Wydawnictwo
Diecezjalne i Drukarnia
w Sandomierzu
www.wds.pl

Table of contents

Beyond Britannia, where the endless ocean opens, lies Orkney.
Orosius, 5th century AD

Orkney
the penultimate islands

Scapa Flow, one of the largest natural anchorages in the world, is a place known to every naval history enthusiast. Geographically, it is a vast body of water protected from the wind and ocean waves by the surrounding islands that make up the Orkney Archipelago. Scapa Flow is therefore inextricably linked to the Orkney Islands, also known as the "penultimate islands" (in this sense the 'last' of the British islands are the Shetlands, located even further to the north) and it is from these that the geographical description of the anchorage area should begin.

Orkney is an archipelago north of the Scottish coast. It has around 70 islands and rocks, of which only 16 are permanently inhabited. Lying at 59° latitude, they are only 50 nautical miles further south than the southern tip of Greenland. The islands extend 30 nautical miles from east to west, the extreme southern islands are 53 nautical miles from the northern periphery. Total surface area of the islands is 974 km², the total length of the coastline is estimated at around 570 nautical miles. The archipelago can be divided into three main parts – Mainland, the North Isles and the South Isles. Orkney has a population of about 20,000 (19,450 according to the 1999 census). This represents a decrease compared to 1914, when the island population was 32,000 people. In the 1960s, the most economically difficult period for the archipelago, the population declined to 17,000. The majority of the population is concentrated on Mainland, where the two largest towns are located: Kirkwall (the capital of the archipelago) and Stromness. Mainland is also known by its Old Norse name Hrossey which meant the Horse Island, or by the name *Pomona*, which stems from a sixteenth-century mis-translation by a Scottish historian

Martello tower on the Island of Hoy. Two such towers erected in 1814, along with Hackness Battery were to form the backbone of the Scapa Flow anchorage defenses. The Napoleonic Wars were soon over, therefore the entire enterprise could be considered a project completed much too late.
(K. Kubiak)

Artifacts recovered from the warships of the German Hochseeflotte *scuttled on June 21, 1919, in the Orkney Islands, stored at Kirkwall.* (K. Kubiak)

and humanist scholar George Buchanan. Earlier Pictish or Celtic names of the archipelago have not survived to our times.

The islands are separated from Scotland by the Pentland Firth. It is 6.5 nautical miles wide between the Scottish mainland and South Ronaldsay Island, but only 2.5 nautical miles between Stroma Island in Scotland and Swona of the Orkney Islands. The 3–4 m tides in the straits produce very strong tidal currents.

The northern part of Orkney, "unrelated" to Scapa Flow, includes the following major islands (from the north): North Ronaldsay, Papa Westray, Westray, Sanday, Fara, Rousay, Eday, Stronsay, Muckle, Green Holms, Egilsay, Wyre, Gairsay, Stronsay and Auskerry. They are all located north of the largest island of the archipelago, Mainland.

The Scapa Flow anchorage is squeezed between the four larger islands: Mainland protecting them from the north, northwest and north-east, Hoy (providing protection from the west and south-west), Burray and South Ronaldsay (protecting it from the east).

Within the anchorages and their approaches there are also Graemsay (between Mainland and Hoy), South Walls, Swona, Switha, Flotta and Calf of Flotta (between Mainland and South Ronaldsay), Fara, Rysa Little and Kava (in the south-west area of the anchorage), Lamb Holm and Glimps Holm (between Burray and Mainland). To the east of Mainland lies a tiny island called Copinsay and, to the south of South Ronaldsay, the islet of Pentland Skerries.

The islands surrounding Scapa Flow are treeless pieces of land with steep hills. The hills of Mainland, peaking at 268 metres above sea level (Ward Hill in Orphir) and Hoy (479 m) protect the vast area snuggled between the islands from the fury of north and west winds. These are frequent – in winter, they blow with up to Force 8 and occur in 13 to 18% of observations, in summer the value drops to 5%, only to increase to 9% in autumn. On average, major storms occur 3–4 times a year, sometimes accompanied by hailstorms.

The Orkneys cannot be called "sunny islands". The average cloud cover throughout the seasons is between 5/10 and 6/10. Nevertheless, there are long periods of cloudless weather in the summer, lasting for up to a week. There are often low-level clouds, taking the form of an extremely dense fog (this phenomenon is known as haar). In the waters surrounding the Orkney, visibility exceeding 5 nautical miles is observed in 83% of cases in summer and 90% in winter.

The anchorage itself is about 27 km long and 25 km wide, which gives it an estimated area of about 700 km². The following entrances lead to the sheltered waters:

1. Hoxa Sound (main entrance) – between Flotta Island and South Ronaldsay, minimum width 1.3 nautical miles, minimum depth of the fairway 32 m;
2. Switha Sound between Flotta Island and Switha (minimum width 0.6 nautical miles, minimum depth of the fairway 29 m) leading further through West Weddell Sound (minimum width 0.5 nautical miles, minimum depth of the fairway 3 m) or Gutter Sound (minimum width 0.7 nautical miles, minimum depth of the fairway 16 m),
3. Cantick Sound between Switha Island and South Walls, minimum width 0.9 nautical miles, minimum depth of the fairway 8 metres) leading further through Weddel Sound or Gutter Sound,
4. Holm Sound (currently blocked up by causeways built during World War II, the so-called "Churchill barriers") which is then divided into:
   – East Weddell Sound between Burray and South Ronaldsoy (original width 0.25 nautical miles, minimum depth of the fairway 7 m),
   – Skerry Sound between Glimps Holm and Lamb Holm (original width 0.3 nautical mile, depth of the fairway 9 m),
   – Kirk Sound between Lamb Holm and Mainland (original width 0.3 nautical mile, depth 12 m),
5. Water Sound between the island of Burray and South Ronaldsay, blocked up by the "Churchill barrier" (original width 0.4 nautical miles, minimum depth 8 m),
6. Hoy Sound (main western exit between Mainland and Graemsay, minimum width 0.5 nautical miles, minimum depth of the fairway 36 metres),
7. Burra Sound between the Island of Hoy and Graemsay, minimum width 0.26 nautical miles, minimum depth 6 m, (sailing through it is hampered by shipwrecks scuttled there during both world wars in order to block the strait).

Tidal heights in the Orkney are up to 3 m and the speed of tidal currents in the straits leading to Scapa Flow is up to 10 knots. The average depth of the anchorage is 36 m, the maximum depth in the Hoxa Sound area reaches 61 m.

The location of the anchorage relative to selected points is described by the following distances from Stanger Head on Flotta Island at the main entrance to Scapa Flow:

- to John o' Groats, Caithness – 11 NM (18 km),
- to Duncansby Head – 12 NM (19.6 km),
- to Dunnet Head – 14.5 NM (23 km),
- to Invergordon on the Cromarty Firth (important anchorage and naval base) – 80 NM (128 km),
- Rosyth on the Firth of Forth (important anchorage and naval base) – 230 NM (270 km),
- Whitehall, London (the office of the Admiralty) – 690 NM (1,100 km),
- Stavanger, Norway – 310 NM (469 km),
- Bergen, Norway – 320 NM (512 km),
- Kiel, Germany (naval base) – 540 NM (860 km),
- Wilhelmshaven, Germany (naval base) – 540 NM (860 km),
- Reykjavik, Iceland – 675 NM (1,090 km).

The waters surrounding Orkney are dangerous. In January, 26 to 32% of observations note waves of 4 m and higher to the north and west of the islands. For the eastern areas this value is in the range of 8 to 22%. In July, waves of such height were noted on average in 3 to 5% of observations in all waters surrounding Orkney.

Owing to the Gulf Stream, Orkney waters are warm and do not freeze. In January and February the water temperature there ranges from 5°C up to 9°C. In August, temperatures range from 12°C to 14°C. In winter, however, high humidity, caused among other things by relatively high water temperature, combined with negative air temperature and strong winds, poses another threat to watercraft – icing of decks, superstructure and rigging.

The first permanent human settlements were established in the Orkney Islands around 5,000 years ago.

In later centuries, successive waves of settlers came to Orkney. It seems that finally the islands found themselves in the Pictish sphere of influence. They were the ones who inhabited the islands when the Vikings came from across the sea at the end of the 8th century. It should be emphasized that Celtic missionaries who evangelized the Picts had arrived in Orkney earlier. The Scandinavian invaders took control of the archipelago with relative ease and made it a base for further trips to the coasts of Scotland and Ireland.

The aircraft carrier HMS Ark Royal *and five of her Swordfish aircraft. The photo was probably taken in the summer of 1939. (NA, ref. 85716).*

N

ATLANTIC OCEAN

PAPA WESTRAY

NORTH RONALDSAY

NORTH RONALDSAY FIRTH

Bay of Noup

Papa Sound

WESTRAY

THE NORTH SOUND

Otters Wick

Start Point

Bay of Lopness

Skea Skerries

Calf of Eday

SANDAY

Faray

WESTRAY FIRTH

Raphess Sound

Sound of Faray

SANDAY SOUND

Saviskaill Bay

Eday Sound

Holm of Huip

Eynhallow

Egilsay

Muckle Green Holm

Linga Holm

STRONSAY

Brough Head

Birsay Bay

Birsay

WYRE

St. Catherine's Bay

Marwick

Gairsay Sound

Sweyn Holm

GAIRSAY

STRONSAY FIRTH

Bay of Holland

MAINLAND

Veantrow Bay

Bay of Skaill

Bay of Linton

Ingale Skerry

SHAPINSAY

AUSKERRY SOUND

WIDE FIRTH

Bay of Firth

AUSKERRY

The String

Shapinsay Sound

Stromness

Kirkwall

Inganess Bay

Hoy Sound

GRAEMSAY

Houton

Deer Sound

Scapa Bay

Waulkmill Bay

SCAPA FLOW

St. Mary's

Bring Deeps

Corn Holm

Copinsay

Cava

Rysa Litte

Call of Flotta

Echnaloch Bay

Hunda

Rack Wick

HOY

Fara

BURRAY

Lyness

FLOTTA

Water Sound

Litte Rack Wick

Sound of Hoxa

Switha Sound

SOUTH WALLS

Switha

SOUTH RONALDSAY

Swona

NORTH SEA

PENTLAND FIRTH

Dunnet Head

Stroma

Gill's Bay

Dunnet Bay

Thurso

Freswick Bay

CAITHNESS

0   5   10   15 Nm

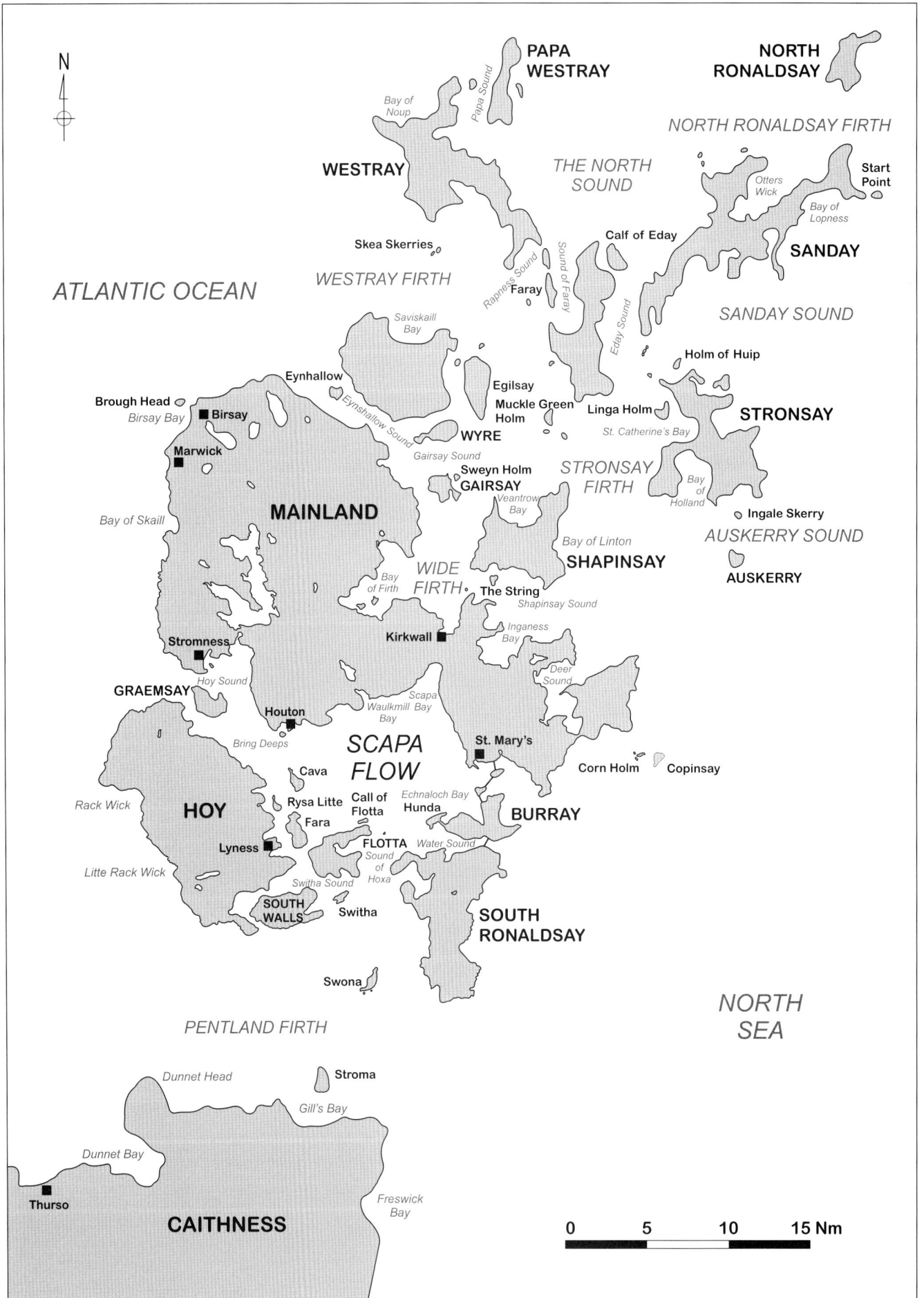

Orkney and Scapa Flow.

The battlecruiser Repulse
with her sistership the
Renown (seen in the back-
ground) were frequent visi-
tors at Scapa Flow. A prewar
photo, taken while the ships
were performing artillery
training (U.S. Naval History
and Heritage Command,
NH 70079, NH 57181).

It could be argued that it was the sailors and warriors from Scandinavia who first saw and exploited the qualities of Scapa Flow as a naval base. They also erected two coastal castles guarding the straits, Paplay overlooking Holm Sound in the east and Cairston, situated near the present day Stromness, guarding Hoy Sound. The seat of the Jarl of Orkney was located in the area of today's village of Bu in the Orphir district, on the south coast of Mainland. To this day the ruins of a round church, built by Jarl Haakon as penance for murder of his cousin and co-ruler Magnus (after canonisation he became the holy patron of the islands), can still be seen there.

Orkney remained part of the Danish-Norwegian crown's domain until 1471. Three years earlier, King Christian I of Denmark had pledged to pay the Scots 50,000 florins, and the Orkney and Shetland islands were offered as collateral. However, since the promised amount was not paid, the Scots seized both archipelagos. Scandinavian cultural influence lasted much longer than the political power of Danish kings. As late as in the end of the 17th century, a local variant of the Norwegian language, known as Norn, was still prevalent in two parishes.

In the Elizabethan era, a ship dropped its anchor at Scapa Flow. On board was a famous mariner, Martin Frobisher, who in 1576 set off towards the shores of North America. Frobisher was chasing a mirage, a north-west passage from the Atlantic to the Pacific Ocean, which was to open the shortest sea route to China and India for the British. According to local tradition, the ships of the Spanish Great Armada, following their defeat in the English Channel, tried to return to their homeland by circling around the British Isles and also reached the area.

An important event as far as the economic and social history of the islands is concerned was the beginning of their ties with the Hudson's Bay Company (operating in northern Canada) in 1702. Until 1891, the ships of the Company called at Stromness every June, recruiting crews and replenishing supplies. As there were times when the Orkney population made up 75% of the company's entire staff, the relationship with the north left a deep mark on people's minds. From the beginning of the 19th century, farming, breeding and contract work for the Hudson's Bay Company began to be supplemented by fishing. Stromness, Holm, Burray and St. Margaret's Hope became the home ports for hundreds of vessels fishing for herring in the North Sea and also processing centres. However, this branch of the local economy was seriously undermined by the introduction of steam-powered trawlers which, once their holds were full, were able to quickly deliver their catch to ports in the south, mainly to Aberdeen. In this changed situation, the salting of herring was no longer necessary and local processing lost its raison d'être.

However, it was not until World War I that the Orkney fishing industry was doomed. Vessels scuttled across the eastern straits were not removed after the war. So even when the threat of mines in the North Sea was removed, the Orkney fishermen had to use the southern exit or the western exit from Scapa Flow and sail around the northern coast of the Mainland to return to their traditional fishing grounds. Both solutions required considerably more time and were also significantly more dangerous.

The Orkney anchorage. The battleship HMS King George V *photographed from the deck of the battleship HMS* Anson. *(IWM, A 13962).*

The Navy enters the stage

For the majority of naval history enthusiasts, both amateurs and professionals, the name Scapa Flow is primarily associated with naval struggles during both world wars. However, the Royal Navy's presence in the Orkney islands dates back to more than a hundred years earlier.

The history of Scapa Flow as a British navy anchorage began in the period of the Napoleonic Wars and the War of 1812. In 1813 the British erected the first fortifications in the Orkney Islands. This was the Hackness Battery on the northern tip of South Walls island, built in 1813, and two Martello towers constructed a year later. The battery remained in its original configuration until 1866, when the threat of war with France led the British to strengthen their coastal defences, neglected after the Napoleonic Wars. Eight 24-pdr guns were replaced by four 68-pdr ones. New battery emplacements and ammunition magazines were built in the old earthwork for the new artillery pieces. Most of the time the battery was manned by a skeleton crew. In 1883 there were only two people responsible for the maintenance of the guns and gunpowder storage. The 68-pounders were fired for the first time only in 1892, when the Orkney Volunteer Artillery Unit held a one-day exercise.

During the First World War, Scapa Flow was the largest and the most important base of the Home Fleet. Following the end of the Great War, it was where the majority of German High Seas Fleet ships met their ultimate fate, being scuttled by their own crews. It was also the time when the base facilities and defensive installations in the Orkney Islands were expanded as necessary.

After the end of hostilities, the Royal Navy began to gradually reduce its presence in the Orkney Islands. Closing of successive military installations was accompanied by the sale of a large part of their

German Hochseeflotte *interned at Scapa Flow. (U.S. Naval History and Heritage Command, NH 94557).*

facilities. In March and April of 1922, the Admiralty auctioned the residential and administrative buildings, erected during the war in Longhope on the island of Hoy, as well as the residential and workshop barracks on the island of Flotta. In the following months, the hydrophone system monitoring station at Stranger Head on Flotta Island, the Caldale Air Station at Kirkwall, the telegraph station at Old Head on South Ronaldsay, the barracks at Burray Ness and St Margaret's Hope, the buildings of the submarine weapons workshop at Hoxa and Cantick, also went up for auction. The British did not intend to mothball or store at weapon depots the coastal batteries erected on Orkney during the war. The guns were put up for auction and sold to local scrap dealers. Another sign of the islands' return to peacetime routines was the suspension of recruitment for local voluntary military formations. That meant an 18-year gap in the functioning of the Orkney Territorial Artillery. While other decisions made by the military authorities to dismantle military installations were welcomed by the majority of the population, this one met with opposition. The Orcadians were certainly not a militaristic community, but the local military formation was part of the local identity and the decision to stop recruitment was a serious blow to the islanders' pride.

Australian heavy cruiser Australia *at Scapa Flow in mid 1940 (U.S. Naval History and Heritage Command, NH 79146).*

Before another war and the first weeks of the struggles

The turbulent 1930s in Germany and the taking of power by the Nazi Party (NSDAP) forced the government and the Admiralty to change their approach to the defence of Britain's largest anchorage. It was only in 1937 that the Navy Command again saw the potential of Scapa Flow in the event of the outbreak of another European armed conflict. A document prepared by the Admiralty, entitled "War Memorandum (Germany)", stated that the main base of the fleet would be located to the north of Rosyth, while it was desirable to organise a manoeuvring base, capable of handling three battleships and two aircraft carriers together with security units, at Scapa Flow. An addendum to the "Memorandum", which examined the possibility of a situation in which Britain would have to face both Germany and Italy, also envisioned the use of an anchorage in the Orkney Islands. In January 1939, in the next "War Memorandum", the Admiralty made it clear that Scapa Flow would be the "fleet base".

In the period of threat assessments, the main burden was shifted from naval units (both surface and underwater ones) to aviation. In 1939 the British Royal Air Force Command estimated that the German *Luftwaffe* would be capable of either carrying out one massive bombing raid against the Orkney Island, using bombers carrying a total of 446 tonnes of bombs, or of carrying out systematic actions against

The British battleships HMS Resolution, Queen Elizabeth, Barham and Royal Oak during joint manoeuvres of the Home Fleet (dark grey hulls) and the Mediterranean Fleet (light grey hulls). Although not seen in the photo, the battleships HMS Nelson and Rodney were probably also participating in the manoeuvres.

Element of the Lyness base
fuel pipeline system.
(K. Kubiak)

the base for a longer period time with planes carrying one-third of the said load. According to the same estimates, 36 heavy anti-aircraft guns had been recognised as necessary to ensure the safety of the base (for comparison it was estimated that Malta would need 72 guns). However, that calculation was based on the assumption that naval ships, both at the base and at sea, would be capable of defending themselves, and the coastal artillery would only protect the logistical infrastructure and auxiliary units. As part of the construction of the anti-aircraft defence system of the base, an air defence radar station was relocated from Ravenscar in Yorkshire to Orkney. That was the final stage in the creation of a system of observation posts covering the approaches to the eastern and northern coasts of the UK.

In the summer of 1936 the Admiralty, bearing in mind the experiences of World War I, surveyed the Hoxa Sound, Switha Sound and Hoy Sound for sites of potential boom barrages. In the same year, construction of a naval fuel depot at Lyness was initiated. That work was done by Balfour Beatty Ltd, which by the end of 1937 had completed several above-ground tanks with capacities of 12 and 15,000 tonnes for a total capacity of 100,000 tonnes of fuel. The process of filling them began in December.

In 1938, construction work was started on the underground tanks that were recessed into the Wee Fea hill in the vicinity of Lyness. The work was done by William Arrol & Co. of Glasgow, a company employing 400 workers, including British and Norwegian miners. However, the work progressed at a snail's pace and the first tank was only put into service in 1942. The other five were completed the following year. They could store 100,000 tonnes of fuel. Until those were filled up, the Home Fleet fuel reserves was stored in surface tanks, exposed to risk of being destroyed.

In June 1938 the position of Boom Defence Officer, Scapa, was created, which was given to Lieutenant Commander J. G. Hopkins. His command post was at Rysa Lodge on Hoy. At that time there were two boom defence vessels and the net layer *Guardian*. Until the Munich Crisis, a boom barrage was laid between Hoxa Head on South Ronaldsay and Quoyness on Flotta Island. As international tension was increasing, Admiral Charles Forbes, the Home Fleet Commander, ordered the subordinate quartermaster services to purchase two concrete barges, *Zata* and *Majda*, from a businessman in Stromness. A tugboat hired from Metal Industries then towed them to Lyness, where they waited to be scuttled as block ships in the Kirk Sound (eventually, five months later, the *Majda* was scuttled, however, not in Kirk Sound but in Water Sound).

The Admiral's decisions were the result of a previously prepared report on the state of the obstructions made up of scuttled ships, which were part of the eastern straits during the previous war. He stated that while the East Weddel and the Skerry Sound were still effectively blocked, the Kirk Sound could be passed through by a vessel of up to 2,000 tons. There was a 120 m wide and 10-12 m deep gap between the wrecks. Therefore, the barges were prepared for being scuttled, but final decisions were not made. It was not until March 1939 that the naval commander of the area (Scapa Flow was territorially subor-

dinate to the Commanding Officer Coast of Scotland – COCOS) reported that on the 15th of the same month the merchant vessel *Serino* was scuttled in the Kirk Sound. However, according to the author of the report, it was necessary to conduct a thorough assessment of Scapa's accessibility through the eastern straits. The mission was performed by the hydrographic ship *Scout*. Her commander's report was reassuring. It stated that it was not possible for a vessel to sail through the Kirk Sound without being exposed to serious risks.

Ultimately, however, any further work on obstructing the straits was temporarily blocked by the accountants. The Department of Treasury granted £10,000 for the purchase of vessels to be scuttled there, while the price of a single vessel suitable for that purpose ranged from £12,000 to £13,000. It was only Admiral Forbes' firm opposition that changed the decision. The amount of £30,000 was allocated for the acquisition of three vessels to be scuttled in Kirk Sound and Water Sound. However, it took some

time to find suitable vessels and the straits were not blocked until the war broke out. The *Cape Ortegal* was scuttled on the bottom of Kirk Sound on 5 September, but the *Lake Neuchatel* was not used as a blockship.

On July 22, 1939, the Admiralty began manning of the Lyness fuel depot. The current operation of the installation and its maintenance and extension required 650 soldiers and contracted civilian workers.

In conclusion, in the inter-war period, successive British governments had been taking by the handful from the "peace dividend" and were extremely reluctant to accept the cost of defence efforts. The result was a serious failure to modernise operational components and reserves of all types of armed forces. In the Royal Navy, budgetary constraints had affected both naval forces and naval aviation, as well as base infrastructure. A glaring example of the latter was the construction of the naval base in Singapore, which dragged on from 1922 to 1938, and desperate underinvestment of the Home Fleet base in the Orkney Islands.

The situation also led the British to reactivate territorial formations in the Orkney Islands. Volunteers from Caithness and the islands formed the 226th Heavy Anti-Aircraft Battery (Territorial Artillery) Orkney and Caithness. It was divided into two half batteries, one stationed on the mainland and the other on the islands. They were armed with 114 mm static anti-aircraft guns. Formation of the battery was completed on May 20, 1938 and as early as July its staff completed their first training as a whole at the Burrow Head training camp in Wigtownshire. Training exercises were repeated the following year. However, the problem was not the lack of trained staff, but in the shortage of equipment. In 1938 at Scapa Flow there were eight 114 mm anti-aircraft guns deployed around the above-ground tanks of the Lyness fuel depot on the island of Hoy. The situation of the coastal artillery emplacements, manned by another reconstructed territorial unit, the Orkney (Fortress) Company, was even worse. It had five guns: two 152 mm in both Ness and Stranger Head, one 120 mm in Neb plus five searchlights.

The construction of defensive installations was somewhat accelerated after the aforementioned designation of Scapa Flow as a "fleet base". A telephone and telex network was developed around Scapa, a telex line connected it with Rosyth. The work at the observation centre at the main entrance to the anchorage (Stranger Head on the island of Flotta) was boosted and completed in August 1939.

An important role in improving the state of defence of the anchorage was played by the Fleet Air Arm, which started the construction of the Hatston Royal Navy Air Station (named HMS *Sparrowhawk* according to naval aviation tradition). Patrol aircraft and anti-submarine planes were to be stationed there in the future. From February to May the runways and aircraft parking spaces were completed, while the work on hangars, workshops and staff buildings continued.

In April 1939, the post of Senior Naval Officer at Scapa Flow (eliminated after World War I), responsible for the protection and defence of the anchorage, was restored. In May, the construction of boom barrages between Scad Head on Hoy and Houton was completed and mooring barrel buoys were anchored at Gutter Sound (between the islands of Hoy, Cava and Little Rysa).

The partial mobilisation in the Orkney Islands began on August 22. When the "Hastings" signal was received, officers of territorial units were appointed and telephone and telex stations were manned around the clock. A few hours later the "Byng" signal came. From the morning hours of August 23,

anti-aircraft artillery and searchlights, as well as coastal artillery units, began to be supplemented up to 60% of their wartime posts. The 226th Battery personnel, mobilised on the mainland, was transferred to the islands aboard the old packet steamer *St Ola*, chartered for the occasion. Coastal artillerymen arrived from Stromness to the island of Flotta aboard two ships chartered by the War Department. In the afternoon of August 23, a general mobilisation was announced.

At that time the Admiralty concentrated the Home Fleet at Scapa Flow. Among the ships which arrived there were the battleships HMS *Nelson*, *Rodney*, *Royal Oak*, and *Ramillies*, the battlecruisers HMS *Hood* and *Repulse*, the aircraft carrier HMS *Ark Royal*, the cruisers HMS *Southampton*, *Glasgow*, *Effingham* and *Enterprise*. At the outbreak of the war four battleships, two battlecruisers, the aircraft carrier, four cruisers, 17 destroyers, eight minesweepers and a dozen or so auxiliary units were anchored there, including the destroyer depot ship *Greenwich*. Apart from those, the old battleship HMS *Iron Duke* was also dispatched to Orkney, arriving there on August 26. Although she was intended to serve as a stationary hulk, she went on patrol (escorted by two destroyers) to the Fair Isle area on October 8.

On August 25, 771 Squadron Fleet Air Arm, equipped with Gloster Sea Gladiator biplanes, arrived at Hatston airfield. Earlier, 700 Squadron, flying Supermarine Walrus flying boats, had been redeployed there. Both naval aviation squadrons were transferred under operational subordination to the RAF. At that time, the Fighter Air Command was at Wick, in the north east of Scotland. It was not until later that a permanent command post was established near Kirkwall, in connection with the increased air force presence in the Orkney Islands.

HMS Renown *with anti-torpedo bulges.*

The landmark of Orkney, a sea stack known as the Old Man of Hoy, which stands on the west coast of Hoy. (K. Kubiak)

Initially, it seemed that the *Iron Duke* would be able to accommodate all the institutions of the base, which was being intensely expanded. However, when the space required by the newly established Admiral Commanding Orkney and Shetland (ACOS) headquarters was determined, it turned out that there would be not enough room to accommodate it (the transfer of the headquarters to the ship did not take place until the second half of October). Therefore, the Admiralty chartered the passenger ship *Voltaire* and dispatched her north. The ship housed some of the military institutions.

On September 1, the ships and base defence forces were on full alert. The war preparations had not yet been completed. As a result of numerous delays, Kirk Sound was not satisfactorily blocked, the anti-aircraft artillery did not have enough firepower, and the 39th Lightweight Anti-aircraft Battery (equipped with 40 mm Bofors guns) assigned to Scapa was still in the Firth of Forth. Boom barrages were far from being completed and no minefields had been laid. To strengthen the anti-aircraft defences of the fuel depot at Lyness, machine guns were removed from ships and sent ashore, together with their crews. Nineteen soldiers and an officer of the 226th Battery, armed with an obsolete Lewis gun from the previous war, were responsible for defending of the Netherbutton radar station. That was the state of affairs on September 3, when Great Britain and France declared war on Germany.

Initially, Orkney was not directly affected by the ongoing conflict. In the first days of September the only sign of that was the fact that Home Fleet spent noticeably longer periods of time at sea. Naturally, wartime readiness was maintained, but the storm of war had not yet loomed over the northern islands. It was believed for a long time that its first herald was a German reconnaissance aircraft spotted on September 5. However, following verification of the records in the battle logs of German units, it turned out that the *Luftwaffe* did not carry out any flights over Orkney on that day. Therefore, the "enemy aircraft" was most probably a mistake on the part of the observers.

In the first weeks of the war, the fate of the base in the Orkney Islands and the Polish submarine ORP *Wilk* (Wolf) intertwined. On September 14, the sub crossed the line of German guard ships at the approaches to the Baltic Straits and crossed the Flint-Rinne channel between Saltholm Island and the Swedish coast. On September 22 (according to British publications a day earlier) the *Wilk*, having successfully sailed thorough the German-controlled eastern part of the North Sea, entered Scapa Flow. The arrival of the Polish ship caused consternation to the British command, as it was not detected even though her course crossed the combat patrol areas of British submarines and surface units. At Scapa, *Wilk* was moored to the side of the depot ship *Greenwich*, where her commander, Lt. Bogusław Krawczyk, received a cabin. The rest of the crew had to live aboard their ship, but used the bathhouse, laundry room, mess hall and other benefits of the depot ship. The ship stayed in the Orkney Islands until October 12, when together with a British destroyer she went to Rosyth and then further to Dundee for repairs (they were carried out by the Caledon Shipyard).

The quiet time period at the Orkneys was spent on frantic expansion of the infrastructure, but due to a lack of military equipment, work was carried out mainly within social facilities. At the meeting of the war cabinet on September 6, it turned out that, indeed, very little can be done to immediately strengthen the defences of the anchorage at Scapa Flow. In the end, it was only agreed to sent 20 barrage balloons withdrawn from London's defences to Orkney. It was also not possible to assign either additional heavy anti-aircraft artillery guns or the two postulated RAF fighter squadrons (the RAF lacked 15 squadrons in full combat readiness to thoroughly secure the country's defence needs) to Scapa Flow.

In September, a forward-looking plan to expand Scapa Flow's defences was also presented, referred to as "Plan Q", which assumed deployment of 80 heavy and 40 light anti-aircraft guns, 108 searchlights and 40 barrage balloons. However, that plan was heavily criticised by Winston Churchill, who once again took office as the First Lord of the Admiralty. In view of the scarcity of resources at his disposal, he considered it unreasonable to engage such a large force in the north, and therefore weaken other areas of much greater importance to Britain. Eventually, the First Lord of the Admiralty accepted the immediate deployment of 16 additional 94 mm anti-aircraft guns and further guns of the same calibre, supported by nine 40 mm Bofors guns, by the end of the year. It should be emphasized that at the outbreak of the war there was no uniform command controlling the forces deployed in the Orkney Islands that were not under control of the navy. For example, the 226th Battery was a part of the 36th Edinburgh Anti-Aircraft Artillery Brigade and the coastal defence troops were under the Scottish Command also located in Edinburgh. To complicate matters further, the navy claimed that both formations were under its operational control. Therefore, on September 29, 1939, the Orkney and Shetland Defences (OSDef) command was established, under command of Brigadier-General Goeffrey Kemp (in January 1943 the command was taken over by Major-General Slater). Initially, only eight guns of the 226th Battery, two 40 mm Bofors guns of the 39th Battery, 275th Engineering Company and a company of the 5th Battalion, Seaforth Highlanders, protected the coastal batteries at Stranger Head and Ness.

In addition to the main anchorage at Scapa Flow, in the harbour of Kirkwall the navy was preparing to organise a command post for the units assigned to the Northern Patrol. They were to carry out the same tasks as the forces bearing the same name during World War I, i.e. to guard the passages between the coast of Norway, Shetland and Orkney leading to the open Atlantic waters, in order to intercept German merchant ships and auxiliary cruisers, control neutral shipping and detect possible attempts made by the enemy's heavy naval units to sneak into the open ocean. The commander of Northern Patrol was Vice Admiral Max Horton, who set up his headquarters at the Kirkwall Hotel, renamed HMS *Pyramus*.

However, the British Northern Patrol organised during World War II was much weaker and more vulnerable to enemy attacks than its counterpart 20 years earlier. Then, the armed merchant cruisers patrolling the frontiers could count on rapid support from detached forces of the Grand Fleet, and the enemy did not conduct a commerce war with heavy naval units. In 1939 the situation was completely different. The British had had a chance to experience that on November 23. It was then that the armed merchant cruiser *Rawalpindi*, patrolling the area between the Faroe Islands and Iceland, was attacked by two German battleships, *Scharnhorst* and *Gneisenau*, trying to break through to the Atlantic Ocean. The commander of the *Rawalpindi*, Captain Kennedy, despite being hopelessly outgunned, decided to fight. It could not last long. The armed merchant cruiser, with no armour, armed with four 152 mm guns without a central fire control system, was literally shot into pieces. Her burning wreck went down together with 270 crew members. Twenty-seven of her survivors were picked up by the Germans and the remaining eleven were rescued by the British.

A monument commemorating the death of Lord Horatio Kitchener. The marshal was killed on July 5, 1916 aboard the armoured cruiser Hampshire. *The ship sank off the western coast of Orkney after after striking a mine laid by the U-75. (K. Kubiak)*

Observation post overlooking Water Sound. (K. Kubiak)

However, the *Rawalpindi's* sacrifice was not in vain. Despite the fact that German warships were jamming the cruiser's radio, the thunder of guns alarmed the British cruisers HMS *Newcastle* and HMS *Delhi*. Both ships made visual contact with the retreating enemy, but the falling darkness and rain made it impossible for them to continue tracking the Germans. A large scale British-French operation aimed at intercepting both battleships failed. However, following the sinking of the *Rawalpindi*, the Germans gave up their commerce raiding mission as they had lost the element of surprise. On November 26 both battleships escaped British detection off the coast of Norway and safely returned to the Baltic Sea.

At the end of the first week of October, service routine was interrupted by the monarch's visit to Scapa Flow. During the First World War King George VI had served on board the battleships HMS *Collingwood* and *Malaya* of the Grand Fleet (he participated in the battle of Jutland), so he knew the Orkney anchorage from his own experience. He arrived at the base on October 6, aboard the cruiser HMS *Aurora*, and visited, among others areas, the Fleet Air Arm base HMS *Sparrowhawk* in Hatston and other units.

In the first weeks of October, soldiers of the 7th Gordon Highlanders Regiment began arriving in Orkney. They were assigned to protect the communications facilities and other installations essential to the defence of the islands. Construction of a command post for both coastal and anti-aircraft artillery positions began and the wired communication network was being expanded.

The British battleship HMS Renown.

Günter Prien's mission

In the early days of September 1939 Admiral Dönitz, Commander of the German submarine forces, demanded all available data on Scapa Flow from the German Naval Intelligence Section. It had to include estimates of defensive measures that could have been taken by the British (with particular emphasis on net and boom defences, as well as on ships scuttled to block the waterways leading to the fleet's anchorage). In addition, the task of preliminary reconnaissance of the Scapa Flow area and collecting navigation data was given to the *U-16* (Type IIB) submarine under the command of Captain-Lieutenant Udo Beherens. The U-boat's commander submitted his report on September 11. He reported that due to an extensive system of obstacles, it would only be possible to penetrate the main entrance to the anchorage (Hoxa Sound) if the booms and nets were accidentally opened. At the same time, he provided valuable information about internal currents in the Orkney archipelago, the navigational aids located there (e.g. Capitan-Lieutenant Horst Wellner of the *U-14*, Type IIB submarine, managed to recognize

Captain Lieutenant Günter Prien in the conning tower of the U-47. The photo was taken upon his return from Scapa Flow. (A. Jarski's collection)

the navigational lights' lighting sequence while he was on a reconnaissance mission in that area). Information on sea currents was particularly important. It was already known that their speed was up to 10 knots, so they could be an insurmountable obstacle for a U-boat, which moving submerged was only able to reach a speed of 8 knots for a limited period of time (about 40 minutes). It is not clear whether, and if so how, the idea of a raid on Scapa Flow was influenced by the aerial reconnaissance of the base conducted shortly before the war. The task was carried out in August 1939 by the military attaché attached to the German embassy in London, Captain Spiller, flying over Orkney in a rented civilian aircraft.

More promising data was provided by first aerial reconnaissance photos of the British base, also received by the commander of the U-boat forces on September 11. Apart from a few heavy units of the Royal Navy they also revealed the system of net barrages in the Hoxa Sound and the obstacles in the form of scuttled wrecks in the eastern and the western entrances. At that time the aerial reconnaissance of Scotland and the Orkney base was conducted by the X. *Fliegerdivision* detached for that task.

Further detailed data concerning Scapa Flow was provided by aerial photos, which reached the submarine command on September 26. During their thorough analysis it was discovered that, although the main and the western entrances should be considered impenetrable by submarines, there was a possibility to pass through the eastern one. It turned out that there was a 17-metre gap between the blockships obstructing Kirk Sound (northern branch of Holm Sound). The depth of water there was seven metres and the shore on both sides was almost uninhabited. It offered an opportunity to pass through, undetected, on the surface at night. Following an analysis of tide charts, it was concluded that the best conditions (highest tide) for the undertaking were expected between October 12 and 14.

Günter Prien was selected to perform that bold task. Dönitz presented the submarine commander with an offer of a raid against Scapa Flow on Sunday, October 1. Prien was the first U-boat commander to whom the commander of the submarine force made an

N

Royal Oak

Pegasus

route of U-47

first torpedo salvo

torpedo from the stern tube

second torpedo salvo

X wrecks

MAINLAND

KIRK

SOUND

LAMB
HOLM

SKERRY SOUND

GLIMS
HOLM

HOLM SOUND

St. Margaret's
Hope

0   1 Nm   2

BURRAY

WATER SOUND

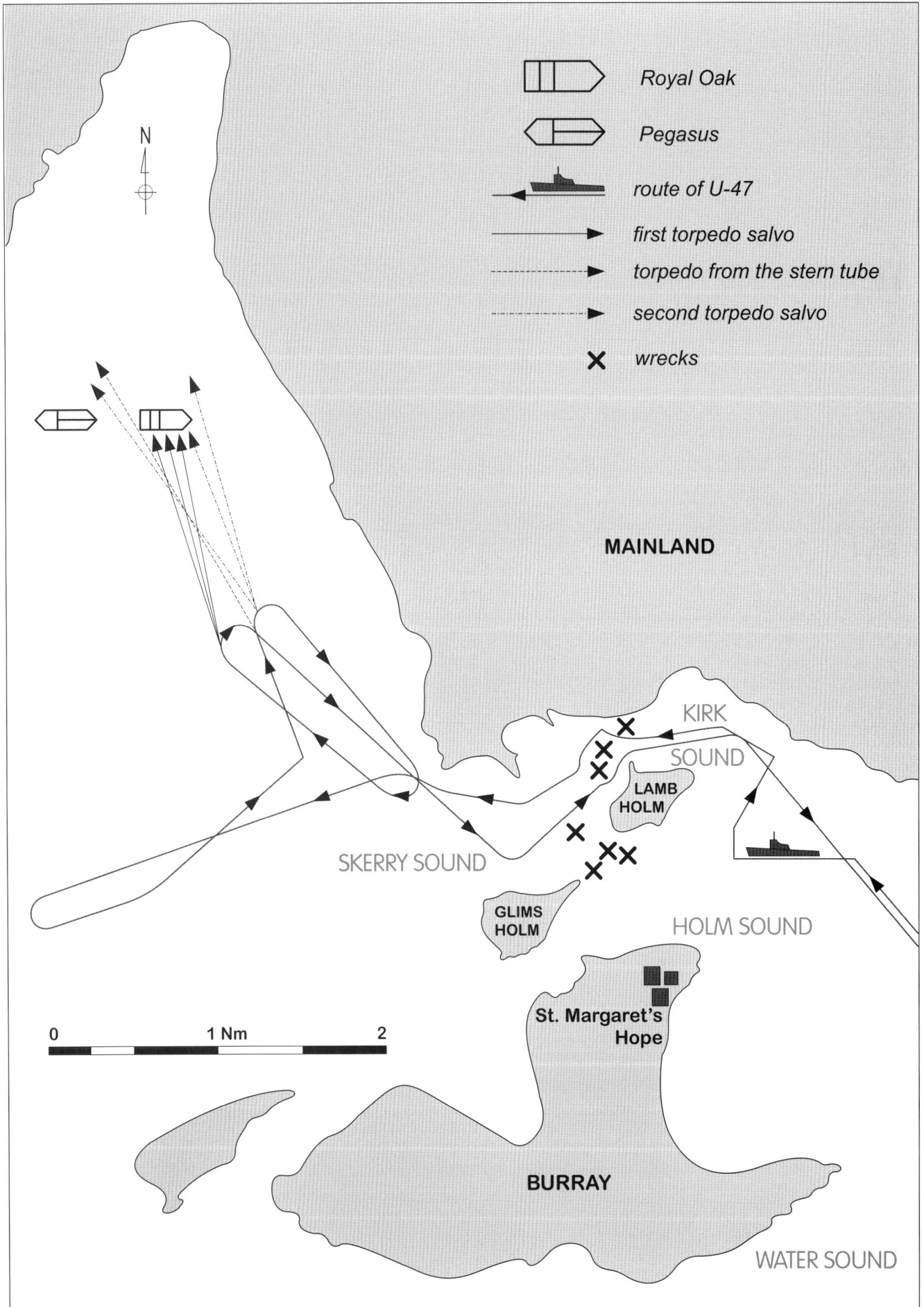

The manoeuvres of the U-47 during the action which resulted in sinking of the Royal Oak.

offer of such a dangerous mission. It can be assumed that such a personnel decision was influenced by the excellent performance of the *U-47* during peacetime training exercises and the fact that Prien, as a former merchant fleet officer, was more experienced and spent more time at sea than most of his colleagues. When talking to Prien, Dönitz made it clear that he needed a volunteer and informed his subordinate that his potential refusal would not have any negative consequences for his further career. The commander of the *U-47* asked for a night to sleep on it and only on October 2, after reviewing the collected reconnaissance data, did he decide to accept the task.

Heading for the Royal Navy base in the Orkney Islands the *U-47* was armed only with Type G7e electrically-powered torpedoes. Since it was strictly an offensive mission, the submarine commander decided not to take any mines on board.

In sending the *U-47* to Scapa Flow Dönitz wanted to achieve the following goals:

He wanted to deliver a serious and painful blow to the Royal Navy, which, in addition to its purely military significance, would have a propaganda aspect and was an important argument in internal discussions and games concerning the priority that should be given to expansion of various branches of the navy.

He also planned to inflict further losses on basic types of enemy warships, by combining the attack on Scapa Flow with laying minefields at the approaches to naval bases which were an alternative to the Orkney anchorage (Sullom Voe in the Shetland Islands, Loch Ewe, Firth of Forth, Firth of Clyde),

Finally, by forcing the Royal Navy to abandon its base in the Orkney Islands, which would result in redeployment of capital ships to Scottish bases, he intended to draw the main forces of the Home Fleet away from the passage between the British Isles and Norway, which was used by German capital ships and auxiliary cruisers leaving German bases for operations against Allied communication lines.

The *U-47*, selected for the operation against Scapa Flow, was a Type VIIB submarine. The initial specifications of these ships were developed in the late 1920s/early 1930s by a secret submarine department of the *Reichsmarine*, camouflaged as *Ingenieursbüro für Wirschaft und Technik*. They were further developed after Hitler came to power. In the course of design work, experience gained during the Great War with Type UB III U-boats was extensively used. The lessons learned during construction of submarines in Finland and Spain, with the help of German advisors, were also incorporated, as well as those learned during construction of the first Type II units. The Type VII prototype vessel went into service in August 1936. However, it soon turned out (especially, in case of the *U-32*, which operated in Spanish waters during the civil war) that Type VII U-boats had insufficient fuel capacity. Therefore, the design was modified by increasing the capacity of the fuel tanks from 67 to 108 tonnes. Such modified submarines were designated Type VIIB. By the outbreak of the war eight of them had been built.

Within four days, the *U-47* crossed the North Sea without being detected by the enemy and on Friday, October 13, moving in a submerged position, reached the far approaches to Scapa Flow. The day before, Prien had received a radio message that there were two capital ships in the base.

It should be noted that the "emptying" of Scapa Flow was provoked by the Germans themselves. On the day Prien took his submarine out to sea, the battleship *Gneisenau* and the light cruiser *Köln* also departed the naval base in Kiel. Both ships headed for the North Sea via the Kattegat and Skagerrak. Their task was to force the Allies to form convoys in that area (thus, their ships could be attacked without notice by the small German submarines operating there) and to lure British capital ships out to sea where they would be in range of the German *Luftwaffe*. On the afternoon of October 8, the German task force was detected by a British reconnaissance aircraft. Then the main forces of the Home Fleet headed into the North Sea with the intention of intercepting the enemy warships. However, on the night of October 9/10 the German ships reversed their course and returned to base on October 10. Earlier, on October

A prewar photo of the U-47. Following the outbreak of the war her white pennant number was removed.

21

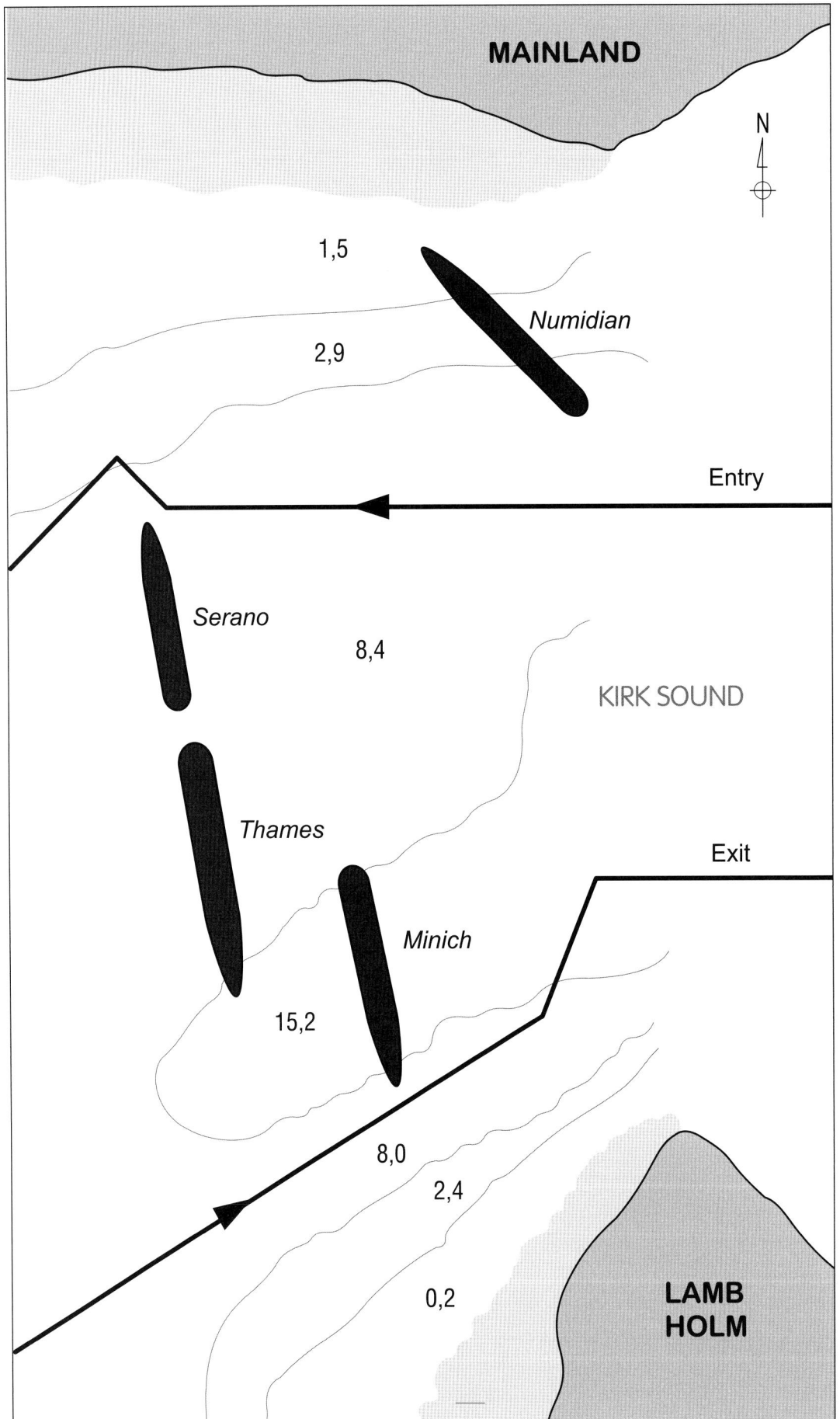

MAINLAND

N

1,5

Numidian

2,9

Entry

Serano

8,4

KIRK SOUND

Thames

Exit

Minich

15,2

8,0

2,4

0,2

LAMB
HOLM

The manoeuvres of the U-47 during her incursion and retreat from Scapa Flow.

Prien's would-be victim, the seaplane carrier Pegasus (ex-Ark Royal). Supermarine Walrus amphibious aircraft being lowered from the deck of the seaplane carrier Pegasus.

9, the *Luftwaffe* had attacked British warships, but none of over 100 bombs dropped by the German aircraft found their mark. When the Home Fleet abandoned the search for enemy warships, the battle-ships HMS *Nelson* and HMS *Rodney*, the battlecruisers HMS *Hood* and HMS *Repulse* and the aircraft carrier HMS *Furious* headed not for Scapa Flow but for Loch Eve in north-western Scotland. Only HMS *Royal Oak* returned to Orkney and joined the seaplane carrier HMS *Pegasus*. The reconnaissance flight performed on October 12 was interpreted by the British command as an announcement of a heavy air raid and therefore a decision to temporarily retain the capital ships in Scotland was upheld. However, the commander of the German submarine approaching Scapa Flow did not know that.

Taking advantage of an early autumn twilight (the sun set at about 19.10), Prien surfaced at 19.15 and started approaching Kirk Strait. The manoeuvring was calculated such that they would reach the blockships in time for high water, which was to take place in four hours time. Natural conditions would support the bold intentions of the *U-47*'s commander. There was a new moon and northern lights were flickering in the cloudless sky. The lighting conditions allowed for recognition of the coastal out-line from the sea, and at the same time made it unlikely for an observer on the shore to spot the low silhouette of the U-boat. At 22.00 the Orkney navigational lights were turned on for 30 minutes (Prien was aware of that owing to the *U-16* commander's report), which made it possible to determine the exact position of the ship (until then there had been various errors in the calculation of the distance travelled). At 23.07, a merchant ship was spotted, so the *U-47* submerged and its commander assessed visibility using the periscope. It turned out that, despite the northern lights, a manoeuvring vessel could not be seen, which would rule out the possibility of attacking the ships anchored at Scapa Flow from a submerged position.

At 23.31 the U-boat surfaced and, carried by the tide, moved westwards. In the darkness Prien lost his way and headed for Skerry Sound. Eventually he realised his mistake, turned the ship to starboard and entered Kirk Sound. Ignoring Dönitz's suggestions, Prien ordered the ship to sail into the central part of the sound, where in aerial photographs he had noticed a wide gap between the hulls of two wrecks blocking the fairway. Having only 13 metres of space between the sides of his own ship and the wrecks, the commander of *U-47* led his U-boat through the "bottleneck", despite rubbing against one of the hawsers connecting the hulls of the scuttled ships with concrete anchors on land. At 00.27 Prien wrote down the sentence "Wir sind in Scapa Flow" (we are in Scapa Flow) in the submarine's logbook. It was 00.27.

Prien and his chief officer were carefully observing the anchorage through binoculars. The first re-sults were extremely frustrating as no enemy warships were spotted and the submarine, manoeuvring close to the shore, was lit by the headlights of a car driving on a coastal road. Luckily for the Germans, the driver did not notice the U-boat. The *U-47* headed north, where the silhouettes of two ships were spotted, which were identified as HMS *Royal Oak* anchored closer to the eastern bank and HMS *Repulse* (a silhouette looming in a distance, further west, which in fact was HMS *Pegasus*). Prien estimated the distance between him and both targets at 3,200 metres and decided to fire a four-torpedo salvo (two torpedoes at each of the enemy ships). At 00.55 the command "Torpedo loss!" was given but only three torpedoes left their tubes. The torpedo in tube 4 (intended for the alleged *Repulse*) got stuck. At that

time Prien was frantically looking at the stopwatch and after 180 seconds, he was disappointed to hear only a single explosion, mistakenly assuming that the *Repulse* was hit. While the torpedoes were being reloading into three bow tubes and the crew was trying to extract the one stuck in the fourth tube, Prien turned the ship and fired a torpedo from the stern tube towards the *Royal Oak*. It missed the target and probably settled on the shore undamaged.

The U-boat commander was extremely surprised that the first explosion did not cause the entire base to be put on alert and decided to take advantage of the situation. The *U-47*, operating on silent and exhaust-free electric motors, made an elongated loop and was again in a torpedo firing positions. At 01.22, three torpedoes left the bow tubes to explode against the side of the British battleship after nearly three minutes. Prien was convinced that this time the torpedoing of the battleship would trigger a response from anti-submarine forces and at 01.28 he began his withdrawal. At that time the *U-47* took the route previously recommended by Dönitz and went through the gap between the northern tip of Burray and the scuttled ships. At 02.15 the U-boat was again in the open sea. At that time the British ship was sinking and there was no chance of saving it.

HMS *Royal Oak* was a Revenge class battleship (*Revenge, Ramillies, Resolution, Royal Oak, Royal Sovereign*, the last two ships of class, *Repulse* and *Renown*, were redesigned and completed as battlecruisers). It was the last class of Royal Navy battleships designed before the First World War. The *Royal Oak* was laid down in January 1914 in Devenport Royal Dockyard, the hull was launched in November of the same year and the ship was commissioned in May 1916. During the Great War the ship was a part of the Grand Fleet and she took part in the battle of Jutland. Following the end of the war, she served both in home waters and in the Mediterranean. During the inter-war period, she was extensively refitted (e.g. her underwater protection was improved by the addition of anti-torpedo bulges). The work carried out also included installation of a catapult and additional anti-aircraft guns.

Following the sinking of HMS *Royal Oak*, the Admiralty held a Board of Inquiry to clarify all the circumstances concerning the loss of the ship. The document was prepared under the leadership of Admiral Drax. According to the Board's findings, at 01.04 (there is a discrepancy in the records – Prien's entry in the logbook states that he launched the torpedoes at 00.55 and the detonation took place after less than three minutes – author's note) there was an underwater explosion on the starboard side of the bow section. Witnesses at the anti-aircraft artillery command post and on the signal platform later testified that a small column of water rose at the bow on the starboard side and splashed on the forward section of the foredeck (the fact that the shock of the explosion was relatively poorly felt and was not accompanied by a high geyser of water could be explained by the use of a torpedo with a non-contact fuse, exploding under the keel and not against the ship's side – author's note). Beams and scantlings were thrown outside from the ship's interior through a hole in the side. In addition, stoppers of the anchor cables were torn off by the underwater explosion. The port side cable ran out completely from its locker and was only held on by the shackle that attached it to the bulkhead. The starboard anchor dropped to the bottom. The explosion and clatter of the anchor chains moving freely in their hawsepipes woke up most officers and some sailors. Rear Admiral Henry Blagrove (2nd Battleship Squadron), who was on board the *Royal Oak*, the ship's commander and the chief engineer ran out on the deck. The officers who were in the aft section were convinced that the explosion was either internal or occurred under the stern as the ship's structure transmitted the vibrations and they were felt more towards the stern.

Then, the ship's commander went towards the foredeck, where he found that the anchor cable stoppers had been torn off and thrown towards the bow. He also listened to the damage reports and sent one of the officers to the lower bow compartments. The Board found out that, at that time, the commanding officer was probably convinced that there was an internal explosion that had occurred in an inflammable liquid store. As the ship was neither listing to starboard, nor trimmed by the bow, the commander went below deck and inspected the interior compartments up to the cable locker. There, he met several officers, among them a senior mechanic, who reported that the ventilation pipe of the inflammable liquid store indicated that there was no fire there and the room was flooded with water. Bottled CO_2 cylinders, used in fire protection systems, which were kept in a compartment adjacent to the store were undamaged.

Until then the possibility of a torpedo hit was probably not even considered. As already mentioned the most likely culprit was an internal explosion or an aerial bomb hit. Upon hearing the chief engineer's report, the commander ordered the pumps turned on and the damaged rooms to be opened, for a thorough assessment of the damage. No order was given to close either watertight doors or portholes.

At that time, Rear Admiral Blagrove was at the stern. One of the staff officers reported to him that the aft section had not been damaged. That information was confirmed a moment later by the chief engineer who, after reporting to the ship's commander, was inspecting the aft compartments. Then the admiral went towards the bow. Following the order of the battleship's commander, the ship's launch and a boat were lowered at that time. They were going to inspect the sides of the bow section. In addition, the *Daisy II* (a mobilised drifter), which served a tender to the battleship, was ordered to raise steam. Moreover, two seamen imprisoned for disciplinary offences were released. Witnesses testifying at the Board's hearing agreed that the ship's crew was not generally concerned about the first explosion. Several sailor even claimed that the explosion had woken them up, but they then went to bed again.

Suddenly, there was another explosion, followed by two more, all on the starboard side, approximately between the main battery turrets "A" and "X". The ship began to heel to the starboard side at once. For 3 or 4 minutes it seemed that the battleship had stopped heeling, but then she lurched over

The victim of Günther Prien's attack, the British battleship Royal Oak. *This prewar photo was taken at Malta. (public domain)*

even faster and at 01.29, 25 minutes after the first explosion and 13 minutes after the second one, she rolled over. Out of 1,200 crewmen, 833 perished.

According to the Board, after the second explosion there was practically nothing that could be done to save the ship. The battleship was plunged into darkness as there was no electricity. Officers in different parts of the ship ordered the seamen they encountered to rescue themselves. The commanding officer was still at the bow, somewhere near the cable locker. He ordered the officers and the seamen to leave the room and he himself went towards the stern, to the dark 'tween deck. He ordered the seamen there to reach the main deck and rescue themselves immediately, then he followed them as well.

The second, third and fourth explosions were also observed by the seamen at the anti-aircraft artillery command post. These explosions were accompanied by columns of water that came crashing down on their position. A flash was seen near the funnel and a lot of black smoke soon enveloped the aft section of the ship. An assistant torpedo officer later testified that following the first explosion he went to the main switchboard, next he went onto the mess deck, where he reported to the chief engineer and then he met an electrician. They all went down to the main switchboard and then to No. 3 and No. 4 generator rooms. Everything still looked normal there. At the time the witness and his companions were in the No. 3 generator room, there was the second, then the third and the fourth explosion. The witness had the impression that the second explosion occurred rather far from his position, in the bow section, the third was near the boiler room and the fourth near the No. 3 generator room, but further towards the bow, probably near the starboard machinery spaces. After the second and the third explosions, orange flames appeared above, in the hatch leading to the generator room, and after the fourth explosion the forward bulkhead of the generator room, between that room and the machinery spaces, began to bulge inward and let the steam through. Two officers and the warrant officer found their escape route upwards almost at the last moment. After a while the lights went out and the flames became less intense. After some time, all three of them found their way to the mess deck. The ship was then listing at about 25° to starboard. The mess deck was filled with choking smoke and burning hammocks.

The Board gathered several accounts from the sailors who were thrown out through doors and hatches into the water by the blasts of the explosions. By the time the ship rolled over, many people had jumped into the water from the fore and quarter decks, but only a few managed to get out from the machinery and boiler compartments. Admiral Blagrove's attitude became the stuff of Royal Navy legend. According to the testimony of one of the stewards, he was on the boat deck when one of the engineers reported to him on his way towards the stern. Then the witness, who himself was taking life rings off the rails on the starboard side, saw the admiral at midship, calling out to the people on the port side to jump into the water from the bow section and to avoid probable injuries by not jumping in the vicinity of the propellers. The steward climbed towards the admiral and asked him to jump with him because

German Type VIIB U-boat, probably the U-47. The photo was taken during the intial phase of the war.

The sinking of HMS Royal Oak *is still remembered. Lord Lieutenant of Orkney, Bill Spencer, laying a wreath at the monument devoted to the victims of the sinking, April 14, 2019. (Tom O'Brien/ www.theorcadianphotos. co.uk)*

he had a lifebelt. The officer refused and remained where he was, helping others to save themselves. He was not seen again.

Meanwhile, the second-in-command of the *Royal Oak*, standing on the foredeck, realised that the ship was listing too fast to conduct any organised rescue operation. The only thing that could still be done was to throw the life rafts (the so-called "Carley floats") overboard and as much wood as possible. Therefore, the commander began doing that with help of several sailors. However, the ship listed very quickly and after a few minutes everyone on board climbed the port side rails, slid down or jumped into the water. The sailors who tried to get into one of the lifeboats on the starboard side had a most frightening experience. They were unable to cut off the rope with which the boat was secured to the davit and they saw the ship "falling on them". Eventually, the tip of the jackstaff hit the boat and it went down. One of the sailors from the said boat was later sucked in by water entering the funnel and then thrown out. Others saw the main battery turrets "A" and "B" rotating and falling into the water.

It was a bitter irony that the second-in-command of the *Royal Oak*, Commander R. F. Nichols, had already experienced a dramatic event at Scapa Flow. In 1917, he served on HMS *Vanguard*, but the night that ship exploded he was on board the amenities ship Gourko, along with a group of sailors, attending a concert organized there by the sailors of the *Royal Oak*...

Given that the ship was in port and the sea was calm, human losses were assessed as very high. The reason for that was that a large number of crew members were under the main (armoured) deck. Their escape from the lower compartments was probably hampered by closed hatches in the watertight bulkheads. It is also likely that, following the first explosion, a number of sailors went into the compartments below the armoured deck, being convinced that they were dealing with an air raid. Their behaviour was in accordance with the rules they had been taught during training.

On 21 October, the cargo ship *Lake Neuchatel* was scuttled in Kirk Sound. Her wreck might have effectively prevented Prien from entering Scapa Flow. Following the loss of the battleship, the Admiralty banned the main force of the Home Fleet from using Scapa Flow. Until the time that development of the defensive infrastructure in the Orkney Islands was completed, Loch Ewe was selected as the main base, while the cruisers of the Northern Patrol operated from Sullom Voe manoeuvring area in the Shetland Islands, which lacked almost all necessary equipment. Thus, one of Dönitz's goals was achieved. The battleship HMS *Nelson* (Loch Ewe, mines were laid by the *U-31*) and the light cruiser HMS *Belfast* (in the Firth of Forth by the *U-21*) were damaged, striking mines laid at the approaches to those alternative bases. Moreover, the Germans, being convinced that the damaged HMS *Repulse* (according to the radio report transmitted by Prien on October 16) would be heading to the nearest shipyard, Rosyth on

Karl Dönitz, already in the rank of Großadmiral *to which he was promoted in 1943. (Bundesarchiv, Bild 146-1976-127-06A / CC-BY-SA 3.0)*

The U-47 *departing for another combat patrol. The new emblem, "Bull of Scapa Flow", can be seen on her conning tower.*

the Firth of Forth, attacked the city with *Luftwaffe* forces, scoring a hit on the light cruiser HMS *Southampton* (the bomb did not explode) and damaging a destroyer. It was the first air strike on a British naval base during the Second World War.

After leaving Scapa Flow, the *U-47* headed south-east on the surface and reached Wilhelmshaven on October 17 at 11.44. Before entering the harbour, her Watch Officer Engelbert Endrass removed the previous informal emblem from the conning tower of the *U-47* (a skull in a top hat with crossbones holding a folded umbrella) with an image of a snorting bull. This "Bull of Scapa Flow" later became the official emblem of the entire 7th U-boat Flotilla "Wegener".

The *U-47* was welcomed by Admirals Reader and Dönitz, standing on the quay. On the deck of the submarine Prien was awarded the Iron Cross 1st Class and all other crew members received the Knight's Cross 2nd Class. Hitler sent his personal aircraft to Wilhelmshaven to take the crew of the *U-47* to Berlin. On the runway of Tempelhof airport the sailors were greeted by thousands of people who had already learned about Prien's feat from radio broadcasts. The crew of the submarine had a ceremonial dinner with Adolf Hitler. During their visit to the Reich Chancellery, Prien received a newly instituted award, the Knight's Cross of the Iron Cross.

Apart from the purely propaganda aspect, Prien's mission played an important role in shaping the future of the German submarine force. It had no direct consequences in terms of the steep increase in the number of submarines being built, but when the surface combatants began to fail or were not successful enough to meet the high expectations, Hitler thought back to U-boats.

The U-47 *returning from Scapa Flow. The submarine passing the German battleship* Scharnhorst.

Prien among his crew. A propaganda photo signed by the commander of the U-47.

Günter Prien already in the rank of lieutenant commander. Able bodied sailor in the foreground is a motorman, while his colleague is a deck hand. (A. Jarski's collection).

Following his success at Scapa Flow, Prien's star was shining brightly. He became a German media hero, a "propagandistically useful" person. (A. Jarski's collection)

Strike from above
and the development of defences

Immediately after the sinking of the *Royal Oak*, the Admiralty decided that the fleet would not return to Scapa Flow. The anchorage was to remain inactive for capital ships until its defences were strengthened to a level that would guarantee the safety of the fleet. Although this decision was taken because of the threat posed by submarines, it probably protected the Home Fleet from the losses that might have been inflicted by the enemy air force.

The idea of an air strike against Scapa Flow was supported by the *Luftwaffe* Commander Herman Göring from the onset of the war. He presented Hitler with a proposal to carry out one massive strike, but the *Führer*, known for his twisted ideas in dealing with Great Britain (he was still hoping for a settlement) refused. German commanders of lower ranks were also convinced of the possibility of attacking Scapa Flow and inflicting serious losses on the enemy.

Scapa Flow in 1939. The former battleship Iron Duke, *now serving as a gunnery training ship, can be seen in the foreground. She was reclassified shortly after the London Treaty came into force. To adapt her for the new role the "B" and "Y" turrets along with torpedo tubes were removed. Those turrets were replaced by 4-inch anti-aircraft guns.*

Orkney as seen from the greenhouse nose of a German Heinkel He 111 bomber of KG 26. (www.scan.ac.uk, ref. 06120011)

The first strike against Scapa Flow took place on the morning of October 17, 1939. It was performed by a force far smaller than those originally requested by the commander of the German air force: four Ju 88A-1 and four He 111 aircraft of *Kampfgeschwader* 30, based on the island of Sylt in the North Sea. The attack was led by Captain Dönch. Apart from auxiliary units, the only ships present at the anchorage were the old battleship HMS *Iron Duke* and the destroyers HMS *Ashanti* and *Eskimo*. German pilots went for the biggest target. Four bombs exploded in the immediate vicinity of the ship. Damaged plating resulted in flooding of the engine room. One crew member died and 25 others were wounded. The *Iron Duke* lost power, the pumps stopped working and slowly, the ship began to sink. The anti-aircraft artillery shot down one of the attacking planes (it crashed in the Pegal Burn area on the island of Hoy) and another was probably damaged. The tugboat St. Martin approached the damaged battleship. She was towed into Ore Bay, where she settled on a sandbank on an even keel. The destroyer HMS *Eskimo* was also involved in the rescue operation, supplying power to the damaged ship. However, she had to

Supermarine Warlus flying boat launched from the deck of the Pegasus *seaplane tender (1942).*

abandon the *Iron Duke* when radar detected another group of enemy aircraft approaching Orkney. This time the raid was carried out by 15 bombers (probably Do 17s) in three groups, of four, seven and four planes each. The accommodation ship *Voltaire* and the coastal infrastructure were attacked at that time, but the bombs did not cause any serious damage. In the late afternoon a single aircraft was spotted over Orkney. It was on a reconnaissance mission to evaluate the results of the air strike.

The sinking of the *Royal Oak* was a shock to the Admiralty and a painful blow to the morale of the nation. Both the Cabinet and the First Lord of the Admiralty were determined to do everything in their power to ensure that a similar event would never happen again. On October 31, Churchill went to Scapa Flow to attend a conference concerning the safety of the anchorage. It was decided to radically strengthen the defences and, by the time the most urgent projects were completed, the Home Fleet was to leave the Orkney Islands. Naturally, these decisions did not mean that Scapa Flow was completely deserted. Capital ships were not based there, but destroyers and cruisers were calling there to refuel. Artillery training was also conducted there by the armed merchant cruiser *Rawalpindi* before she left on her final voyage.

It should be noted that after the Home Fleet left Scapa Flow as a direct consequence of Prien's raid and the sinking of the *Royal Oak*, the work carried out so far to put the army's "Plan Q" into effect came practically to a halt. The reason for that was a lack of clarity as to the future fate of the Orkney anchorage. Resolution of these doubts at the beginning of November restored the previous pace of work.

At that time, three "small stone sloops-of-war" appeared in the landscape of the base, i.e. shore installations named according to the Royal Navy's tradition: HMS *Proserpine* that was the Lyness base,

HMS Norfolk *during her visit in Canada in 1932. On March 16, 1940, while at Scapa Flow, the ship was damaged by the aircraft of* Kampfgeschwader *26. (https://www.naval-history.net)*

Winston Churchill during inspection on Orkney in mid September 1939. The First Lord of the Admiralty is accompanied by his daughter Mary and the commander of the battleship Nelson, *Captain Sir Geoffrey John Audley Miles. On the deck of that warship the British politician sailed to Loch Ewe in north-west of Scotland.*

HMS *Pomona*, the headquarters of the commander in charge of the boom defence nets and minefields and HMS *Pleiades*, the base controlling the drifter pool.

In November, the commander of the beached *Iron Duke* took over as chairman of the Inter-Services Committee for the Defence of the Fleet Anchorage of Scapa Flow. Apart from him, that body was formed by the most senior commanders of the air forces and ground troops deployed on the islands. In December, the Committee presented a plan to strengthen the defences, codenamed "Plan R", extending the scope of projects provided for in the previous "Plan Q". It proposed, among other things, increasing the number of coastal batteries and doubling of boom barrages and remotely-controlled minefields with a hydrophones system. In December, after some corrections, the plan was adopted for implementation. That was in parallel with the change at the post of ACOS, where Admiral French was replaced by Vice-Admiral Binney. A new command post of Rear Admiral in charge of HM Dockyard Scapa Flow was also created (the first one being Rear Admiral Lumley Lyster). His duties were that of a flag officer at the harbour of Scapa Flow (harbour superintendent) and the superintendent of the Lyness naval base. He was also responsible for organisation and supervision of the development of all naval defence installations at Scapa Flow and Lyness. Until August 1940 this position was held by the afore-mentioned Rear Admiral Lyster. It was later taken over by Rear Admiral Patrick Macnamara.

Recruitment of workers was a major problem during construction work. Since Orkney could not provide enough labour, workers from the elsewhere were recruited and offered very attractive rates. A significant proportion of the workers were Irish, both from Ulster and the Republic of Ireland. Their presence heightened the fears of Irish Republican Army infiltration, which, not without reason, was accused of cooperating with German intelligence. Therefore, when anti-British publications were found in one of the barracks, the Irish were banned from the Orkney Islands (as was the case during World War I, they were considered a "restricted zone" since November 21). That issue was partially resolved, under martial law, by the introduction of administrative work orders in the Orkney Islands. The mandatory period lasted six months. However, the situation was radically improved only by the arrival of the 1st Royal Marine Labour Battalion on the islands, a de facto well-equipped road and bridge-building unit. The tasks performed by its soldiers until 1942 (it was only then, that the army was replaced by civilian workers) went far beyond the engineering routine. In addition to building roads, barracks, cinemas and canteens, they also harvested hay for pack mules evacuated from Norway, served as lighthouse keepers in two lighthouses, performed guard duties, watched over a U-boat crew saved by patrol seaplanes, and took part in the rescue operation of the freighter *Tennessee*, when she ran aground on a sandbank near Kirkwall.

Flag Officer, Orkneys and Shetlands (1939–1942) Vice Admiral Hugh Binney. A later period photo shows Binney in the rank of Admiral, when he served as the Governor of Tasmania. (State Library of Tasmania)

Command tower and the searchlight post of Battery Wellington overlooking Shapinsay Sound. It was armed with three twin 57 mm guns. (K. Kubiak)

Wrecks, minefields
and hydrophones

During winter storms, the problem of the effectiveness of the barriers created with scuttled ships in the eastern straits arose again. Heavy storms and hurricane winds upturned and pushed ashore the wreck of the ship *Cape Ortegal* of 4,896 GRT (therefore, quite a large vessel), sunk a week after the war broke out. In Skerry Sound a gap formed again between the wrecks allowing for entrance into the anchorage. In February 1940 stormy waters broke another gap in the barriers, moving another wreck several hundred metres into the anchorage. The situation was aggravated by the fact that two vessels dispatched north and meant to be sunk as blockade ships, the freighter *Pandora* and passenger liner *Durham Castle* of 8,000 GRT, owned by Union Castle, never reached their destination. They both struck magnetic mines and sank in the Invergordon area. It was then proposed to use the refloated wreck of the battlecruiser *Derfflinger*, which remained in vicinity of the *Iron Duke*. However, this idea was scratched, mainly because of the difficulty in reducing the draught of the wreck to the extent that would make it possible to tow it into the strait. Instead, in December 1939, the 5,000 GRT *Gambhira* was sunk in Kirk Sound. Then, in February 1940, despite the negative experience with small ships, the 3,000 GRT freighter *Redstone*, and then in May the 8,212 GRT *Ilsenstein* were sunk as block ships. The latter replaced the *Cape Ortegal*. In addition to the sensitive Kirk Sound, Water Sound also caused problems, where winter storms pushed the wreck of the *Gondolier* into deep water. It was replaced by the *Collingdoc*.

The ships were scuttled on behalf of the Admiralty by Metal Industries, but the company retained its civilian status and avoided militarisation. In July 1940, it took over the responsibility for all rescue and block ship barrier work. In total, vessels of more than 70,000 GRT were sunk in the smaller straits leading to Scapa Flow during World War II. The largest of the block ships was sunk as the last. She was the *Inverlane*, located in Burra Sound between the islands of Hoy and Graemsay.

The "Churchill barrier" between Burray and Glimps Holm (it crosses Weddel Sound). Remains of the Reginald, *one of the ships scuttled to block the Eastern Sounds, can be seen in the foreground. (K. Kubiak)*

Wrecks scuttled in Orkney to block the Eastern Straits.

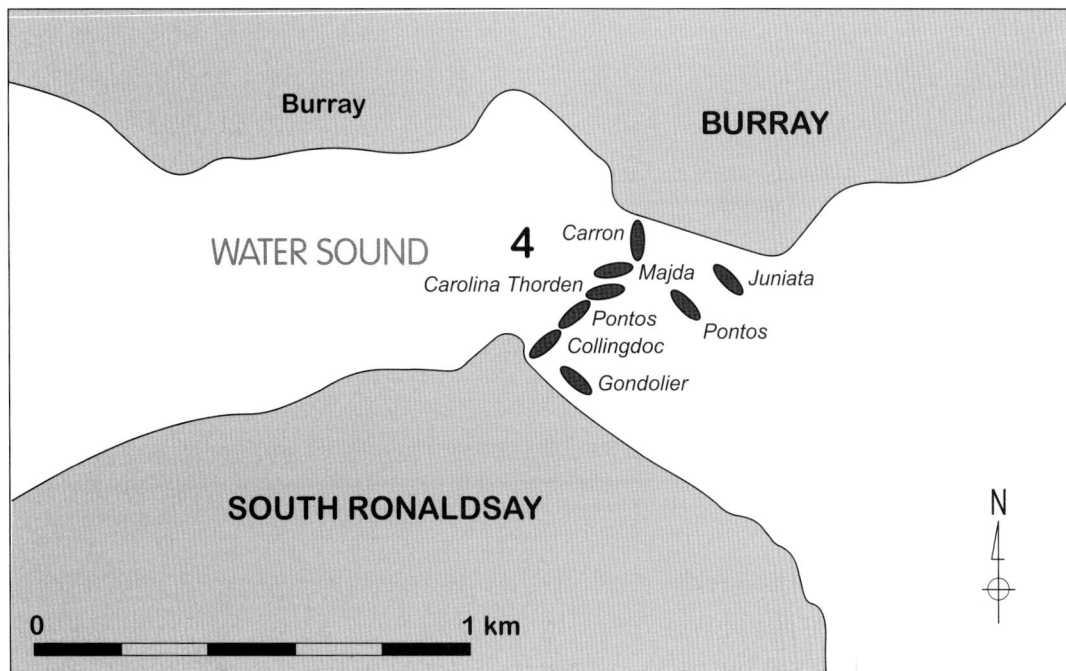

MAINLAND

St. Mary's

Numidian

Serano   Gambhira

1   Lake
Thames   Neuhatel   KIRK SOUND

Minich   Redstone

Busk   Aorangi

ST. MARY'S BAY   LAMB
                              HOLM

Rosewood

SKERRY SOUND   Lycia   Teeswood
                  2 AC.6   Cape Ortegal
                         Ilsenstein   Elton   Rheinfield
                  Almeria
          Emerald Wings   F/C Pontoon
                         Argyle

GLIMS
HOLM

                              EAST WEDDEL SOUND   N

          Lapland

Gartshore   **3**
Empire   Reginald
Seaman
Martis   BURRAY

                                        0   1 km

Burray   BURRAY

WATER SOUND   **4** Carron

          Carolina Thorden Majda   Juniata
                         Pontos
                  Collingdoc   Pontos

                  Gondolier

          SOUTH RONALDSAY   N

0   1 km

35

SHIPS SCUTTLED DURING THE GREAT WAR AND THE SECOND WORLD WAR TO BLOCK THE EASTERN STRAITS LEADING TO SCAPA FLOW				
Name	Tonnage [RT]	Place and date of construction	Year of scuttling	Notes
Kirk Sound – Barrier No.1				
The Great War				
Numidian	4 836	Glasgow 1891	1914	Refloated and sunk again
Thames	1 327	Glasgow 1887	1914	
Aorangi	4 268	Glasgow 1883	1914	
Minich	2 809	Glasgow (?)	1915	Refloated and pushed to the south
The Second World War				
Busk	3 670	North Shields 1906	1940	
Gambhira	5 257	Sunderland 1910	1939	Refloated in 1943, used as target and scuttled again
Lake Neuchatel	3 859	Sunderland 1907	1939	Refloated in 1948
Redstone	3 110	West Hartlepool 1918	1940	Refloated
Seriano	3 543	Michigan	1939	Refloated
Tabarka (ex – Pollux)	3 624	Rotterdam 1909	1941	Refloated in 1944 and scuttled again in Burra Sound
Skerry Sound – Barrier No. 2				
The Great War				
Rosewood	1 757	Siuth Shields 1889	1915	
Teeswood	1 859	(?) 1882	1914	
Elton	2 461	West Hartepool 1880	1915	
Rheinfeld	1 634	Newcastle 1893	1914	
Almeria	2 418	Sunderland (?)	1915	
Argyle	1 118	Hull (?)	1914	
The Second World War				
Lycia	2 338	Glasgow 1924	1940	
Ilsenstein	1 508	Kiel 1898	1940	
Cape Ortegal	4 896	Glasgow 1911	1939	
Emerald Wings	3 139	Cherbourg 1920	1940	
F/C Pontoon (floating crane)	---	----	1941	
A.C. 6. (barge)	--	---	1941	
East Weddel Sound – Barrier No. 3				
The Great War				
Lapland	1 234	Dundee 1890	1915	
Raginald	930	Glasgow 1878	1915	
Gartshore	1 564	South Shield 1880	1915	
The Second World War				
Empire Seaman	1 921	Lubeka	1940	
Martis	2 483	South Shields 1894	1940	
Water Sound – Barrier no. 4				
The Great War				
Lorne	1 186	Hull 1873	1915	
Pontos	2 265	Glasgow 1891	1914	
The Second World War				
Carron	1 017	Dundee 1894	1940	
Colligdoc	1 780	Ontario 1925	1942	
Gondolier	1 730	Glasgow 1866	1940	
Carolina Thorden	3 645	Turku (Finland) 1938	1942	Under Swedish flag, damaged in the Faroe Islands
Juanita	1 139	Sunderland 1918	1940	
Majda (Naja?, concrete barge)	---	---	1939	

Burra Sound				
The Great War				
Gobernador Boris	2 332	West Harpool 1882	1915	
Budrie	2 252	Glasgow 1882	1915	
Rotherfield	2 831	West Hartpool 1889	1914	Blown up in 1961
Ronda	1 941	Sunderland 1889	1915	
Granfe	3 423	Balfast 1894	1914	
The Second World War				
Inverlane	9 141	Vegesack	1944	Bow section used for repairs of another ship damaged by a mine. Only the stern section was scuttled
Tabarka	See Rarier No. 1			
Doyle	1 761	Troon	1940	

However, it was laying of minefields and deployment of a hydrophone system in the Hoxa Sound that essentially strengthened the defence system of the main entrance to the anchorage against submarines. In December 1939, a stockpile of naval mines and hydroacoustic equipment was delivered to Scapa Flow. By the end of the year the ships *Manchester City*, *Miner* and *Ringdove* laid a minefield which comprised eight lines of mines (each mine contained about 250 kg of explosive), supervised by two lines of hydrophones. The mines could be detonated electrically from the control station located in Quoyness on the island of Flotta. The Hoxa Sound minefield was armed on January 21, 1940. The next stage was to lay minefields in Switha Sound and Cantick Sound. They comprised three lines of mines controlled from the station on Stanger Head. The minefields reached combat readiness on February 22, 1940. Then minefields were laid in Hoy Sound to secure the anchorage from the western side (this task was performed by the minelayer *Atrens*). Moreover, the density of mine lines in the Hoxa Sound was increased. By May, a minefield between St Mary's Hope and Burray Island (to be more precise, between Howequoy Head on Mainland and Swannies Point on Burray) had been laid and wreck barriers were doubled. It closed three of the four eastern straits (except Water Sound). A line of mines was also placed in Kirk Sound in front of the wreck barrier. These minefields were controlled from a station at St Mary's Hope, which was completed in May 1940.

Naturally, in the conditions of the Orkney Islands (storms, tides and tidal currents) it was relatively common for the mines to move within the remotely controlled minefields or even to be completely destroyed. In such cases, gaps in the minefields were filled by new ones laid by two specially adapted mining depot ships, *Helvig* and *Alca*.

Anti-submarine protection of the base used by the Northern Patrol (during the Second World War the British also used the name Contraband Control) cruisers and armed merchant cruisers was also a huge problem. Patrol units were based at Kirkwall, on the north-eastern coast of Mainland, outside Scapa Flow. As mentioned before, the Patrol Headquarters had been located at the Kirkwall Hotel since September 16, 1939, which was renamed HMS *Pyramus*. When the ships began to manoeuvre on the watch line, in addition to cruisers, there were also ships brought to Kirkwkall for detailed inspection.

Initially, there were attempts to secure the anchorage area by boom barrages, but that ended in a fiasco. Tidal currents and high tides also thwarted the construction of net barrages. Another boom barrage placed between Redwick Head on the east coast of Mainland and Fit o'Shapinsay to close String Bay was also destroyed after only a few months. The hydrophone chain between Readwick Head and Hacksness on Shapinsay Island and another between Galtness on the opposite shore of Shapinsay and Gairsay Island was finally laid. The latter closed the northern entrance to the anchorage. Hydrophones were then complemented by minefields remotely-controlled from the shore. The work was completed in 1943, which coincided with the decommissioning of HMS *Pyramus*. The North Patrol had ended its operations even earlier, in May 1942.

The ships Lycia *and* Ilsenstein *scuttled to block Skerry Sound. At land preparations are being made to launch the construction of one of the "Churchill barriers". (xray-mag.com)*

Coastal artillery, anti-aircraft artillery and barrage balloons

While minefields and a hydrophone networks basically solved the problem of underwater infiltration, coastal artillery was crucial to stop any potential incursion by enemy surface units. As mentioned earlier, Scapa Flow entered the war with only three coastal guns. Work on new batteries began simultaneously at several locations at the end of November 1939. That included both the construction of new artillery emplacements and searchlight positions, as well as social facilities for the staff. However, the progress of those works was relatively slow. Until June 1940, there were only 19 guns at their positions (six 152 mm in three two-gun batteries, three 120 mm guns, a single one and a two-gun battery, ten 76.2 mm batteries, two single ones and two quadruple ones). Still, the construction of new installations continued, especially after after the German occupation of Norway, as the British believed the threat of motor torpedo boat attacks against the ships at the anchorage was now real. The main emphasis was therefore placed on increasing the density of artillery fire by installing 57 mm quick-firing guns in the newly constructed twin emplacements. Consequently, when the twin emplacements were installed in the Balfour Battery, they were able to fire 400 rounds in three minutes towards Hoxa Sound. That was the amount of time in which the enemy motor torpedo boats would remain in their field of fire, while forcing the strait at 30 knots.

Gun emplacement of twin 57 mm guns. (K. Kubiak)

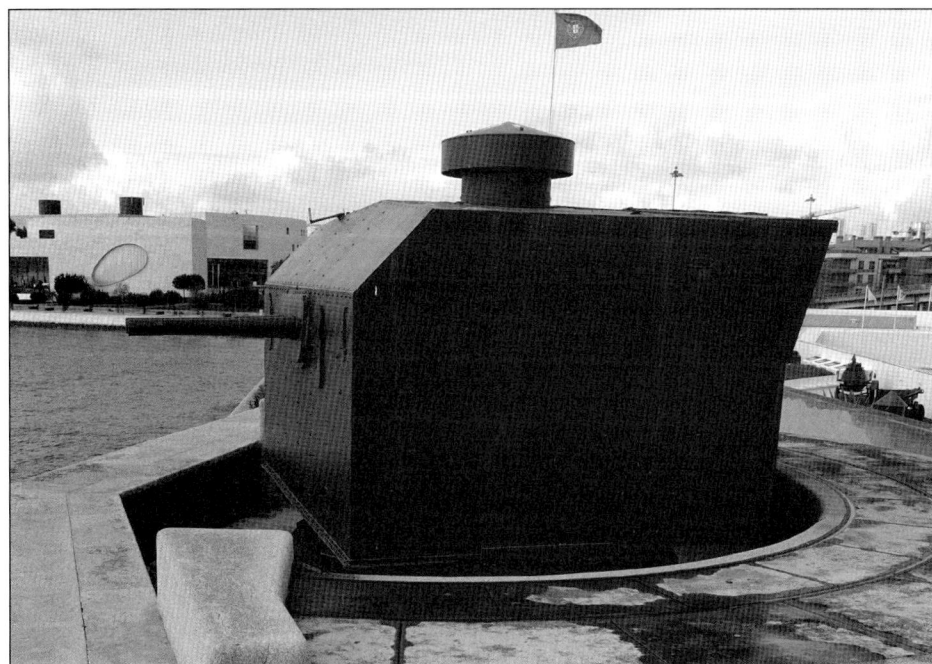

Twin 6-pounder (57 mm) Quick Firing gun turret. That particular one survived at Lisbon. (K. Kubiak)

No.	Name	Location	Active duty	Armament and equipment
				ORKNEY COASTAL BATTERIES DURING THE SECOND WORLD WAR
1	Ness No. 2	Stromness	1938 – 1955	2 x 6" 2 x 90 cm searchlights
2	Links	Stromness	1940 – 1955	July – October 1940 2 x 12-pdr, later 1 x II 6-pdr 3 x 90 cm searchlights
3	Houton	Houton Head	1940 – 1950	2 x 12-pdr 3 x 90 cm searchlights
4	Wasswick	Rendall	1940 – 1945	2 x 12-pdr 2 x 90 cm searchlights
5	Galtness	Shapinsay	1940 – 1950	May 1940 – March 1941 – 1 x 12-pdr, later 1 x II 6 pdr 2 x 90 cm searchlight
6	Castle	Shapinsay	1941 – 1949	2 x 4.7" 2 x 90 cm searchlights
7	Wellington	Carness	1940 – 1945	3 x 6" 4 x 90 cm searchlights
8	Carness	Carness	1941 – 1946	2 x 12-pdr 4 x 90 cm searchlights
9	Rerwick	Rerwick Head	1940 – 1950	From June 1940 until April 1941 2 x 4.7", later 2 x 6" 2 x 90 cm searchlights,
10	Deerness	Mainland	1941 – 1944	1 x 12-pdr 2 x Lyon Light searchlights later 1 x 90 cm searchlight
11	Holm (Clett)	Mainland	1940 – 1944	2 x 12-pdr 1 x II 6-pdr 4 x 90 cm searchlight
12	Lamb Holm	Lamb Holm	1941 – 1944	2 x 12-pdr 2 x 90 cm searchlights
13	Burray	Burray	1940 – 1943	March – July 1940 – 1 x 12-pdr, July 1940 – February 1941 – 2 x 12-pdr later 2 x II 6-pdr 3 x 90 cm searchlights
14	Cara	Cara	1940 – 1944	2 x 12-pdr 2 x 90 cm searchlights
15	Balfour	South Ronaldsay	1940 – 1950	Since May 1940 until March 1941 – 2 x 12-pdr, later 2 x II 6-pdr 2 x 90 cm searchlights
16	Hoxa	South Ronaldsay	1939 – 1950	2 x 6" 2 x 90 cm searchlights
17	Buchanan	Flotta	1940 – 1950	Since March1940 until January 1941 – 2 x 12-pdr, later 2 x II 6-pdr 4 x 90 cm searchlights
18	Stanger	Flotta	1938 – 1950	2 x 6" 1 x 4.7" 3 x 90 cm searchlights
19	Gate & Neb	Flotta	1941 – 1945	2 x 12-pdr 3 x 90 cm searchlights
			1941 – 1950	1 x II 6-pdr 3 x 90 cm searchlights (shared with battery Gate)

20	Innan Neb	Flotta	1940 – 1944	1 x 4.7" 2 x 90 cm searchlights
21	Walls	South Walls	1943 – 1948	1 x II 6-pdr 4 x 90 cm searchlights
22	Scad	Hoy	1940 – 1950	Since June 1940 until August 1941 2 x 12-pdr, later 1 x II 6-pdr 2 x 90 cm searchlights
23	Skerry	Hoy	1940 – 1950	2 x 12-pdr 2 x 90 cm searchlights
24	Graemsay	Graemsay (Point of Oxan)	1943 – 1950	1 x II 6-pdr 4 x 90 cm searchlights

The increase in the number of guns necessitated organisational changes to improve the command and administration of coastal artillery. First, three batteries were organised: 191st Heavy Battery, including emplacements at Stromness, Carness near Kirkwall, Houton, Holm, Wasswick and Shapinsay; 198th Heavy Battery with emplacements at Stranger Head, Neb, Buchanan, Gate on Flotta Island and Scad on Hoy Island; and 199th Heavy Battery located at Hoxa on South Ronaldsay, Balfor, Cara and Burray. Batteries were later transformed into three regiments, called "coast regiments" in the original British nomenclature. These were: 533rd Southern Defence Regiment with headquarters on Flotta Island, 534th Western Defence Regiment with headquarters in Stromness and 535th Eastern Defence Regiment with headquarters in Kirkwall.

In November 1939, following the *Luftwaffe* raids against Scapa Flow, the plan to deploy a total of 80 heavy and 40 light anti-aircraft guns, 108 searchlights and 40 barrage balloons in the Orkneys was approved. All anti-aircraft defence detachments were to be ready for combat by March of the following year, when the fleet was scheduled to return to Scapa Flow. Preparation of anti-aircraft artillery emplacements was more difficult than development of coastal batteries. The guns were mounted in dispersed emplacements, which had to be connected by telephone lines to ensure effective and centralised command. It was also necessary to build a road to each emplacement, not to mention erecting residential and social facilities for the staff. The situation was similar with regard to the searchlight posts. A total of 35 anti-aircraft gun emplacements, scattered around Scapa Flow, were built, as well as 41 searchlight positions. Equipment and armament began arriving in January 1940, when the ships *Cyprian Prince* and *Rutland* anchored at Scapa Flow.

The following units were redeployed to Orkney: 64th Heavy Anti-Aircraft Artillery Regiment from Tyneside, 70th Heavy Anti-Aircraft Artillery Regiment from Merseyside and 95th Heavy Anti-Aircraft Artillery Regiment from the Midlands, the other gun sections of the 39th Light Anti-Aircraft Battery (two guns were moved to Scapa Flow in early September), 142nd Light Anti-Aircraft Battery, 61st Searchlight Regiment from Kingsley, 62nd Searchlight Regiment from Preston. In February 1940 the anti-aircraft defences had 28 heavy anti-aircraft guns in full combat readiness and two light ones. Four more heavy

Ground crew of a barrage balloon at Hoy. (Orkney Library and Archive)

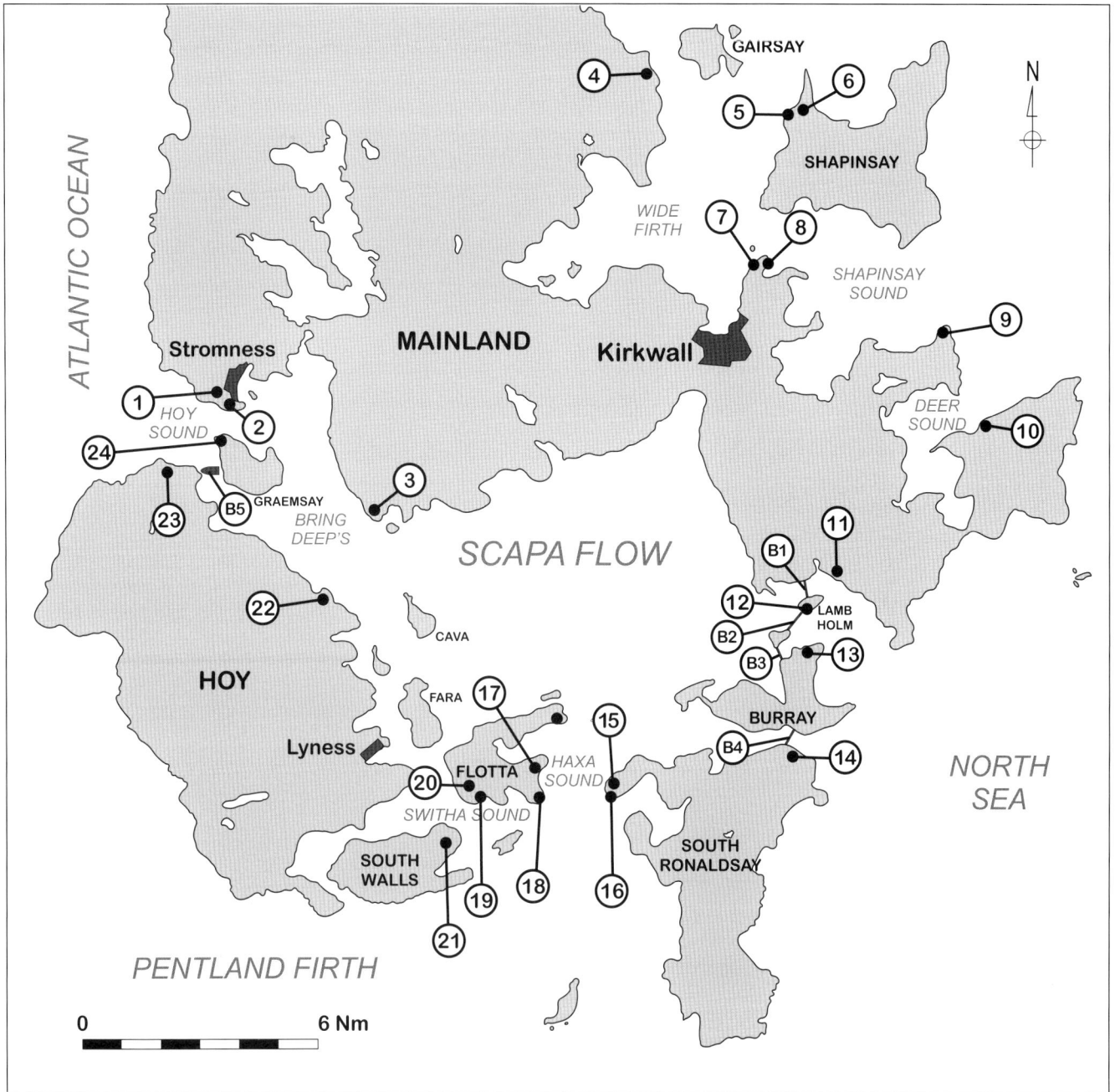

Orkney coastal batteries during World War II.

1. Ness no 2,
2. Links,
3. Houton,
4. Wasswick,
5. Galtness,
6. Castle.
7. Wellington,
8. Carness,
9. Rerwick,
10. Deerness,
11. Holm (Clett),
12. Lamb Holm,
13. Burray,
14. Cara,
15. Balfour,
16. Hoxa,
17. Buchanan,
18. Stranger,
19. Gate & Neb,
20. Innan Neb,
21. Walls,
22. Scad,
23. Skerry,
24. Greamsay.
B1, B2, B3, B4. Churchill barriers,
B5. Wrecks in the Western Straits

guns and 15 light ones were already on the islands, but had not yet been deployed. In parallel with the gun emplacements, an anti-aircraft defence command post was being built, since without it the considerable potential of the firing assets deployed in Orkney could not have been used. It was located near Deerness Road on the outskirts of Kirkwall. The command post reached combat readiness on February 10, 1940. Over the next two months, the process of strengthening the anti-aircraft artillery firepower was significantly increased. On April 15, 1940, 24 hours before the last large scale German air strike against Scapa Flow and the ships participating in the Norwegian campaign anchored there, 80 heavy 114 mm and 94 mm anti-aircraft guns (eight more had not yet be deployed), 32 out of 36 delivered 40 mm guns, 88 searchlights (another six hand not been deployed and 14 stored in warehouses were in reserve) were at full combat readiness.

An essential component that would strengthen anti-aircraft defences were fire-control radar stations that would complement anti-aircraft artillery deployed in the Orkney Islands. The first four emplacements were equipped with such devices at the end of 1940. The radars were also used for directing searchlights.

Between 1942 and 1943, a number of changes were made to anti-aircraft artillery positions, mainly due to the need to provide direct defence for the new air force bases. The year 1943 was also the time of the first reductions in anti-aircraft artillery assets deployed on the islands. As early as April, when the days grew longer, two searchlight batteries were sent back to the mainland. There were not replaced by other detachments.

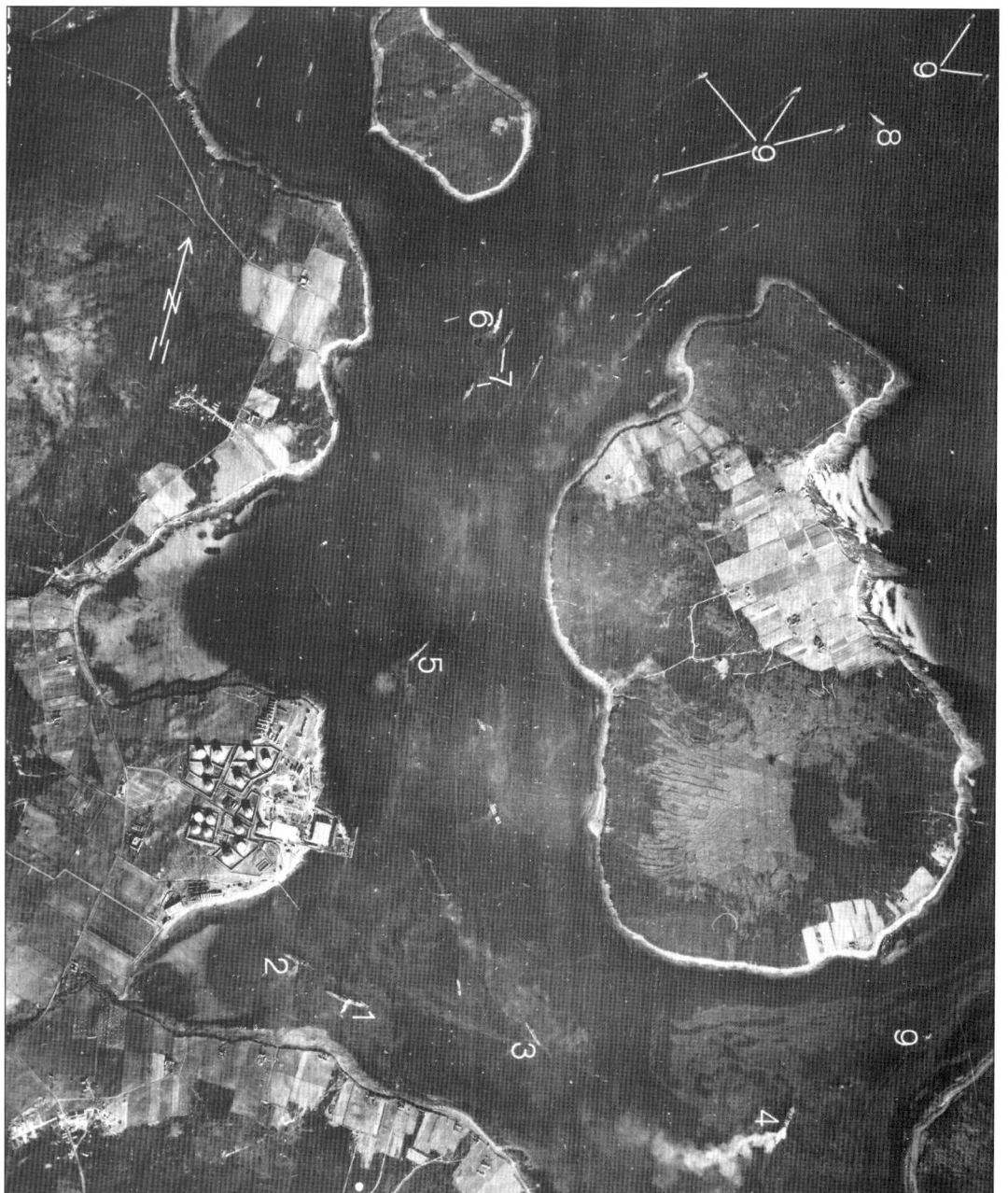

Aerial photo of Lyness taken on October 18, 1939, by the Luftwaffe *reconnaissance aircraft. A pair of fuel tanks is clearly visible. (Bibliothek für Zeitgeschichte, Stuttgart)*

As already mentioned, the plans also called for deployment of barrage balloons in Scapa Flow. The detachment responsible for that type of equipment was 950 Squadron formed at the end of 1939 at 18 RAF Balloon Training Centre in Glasgow. The main force of the squadron arrived in Orkney in January 1940. The balloons were deployed as follows: twelve on the east coast of the island of Hoy, four each on the islands of Flotta and Fara, and eight were to be towed by drifters manoeuvring in the eastern part of the anchorage. The drifters were based at St. Mary's Hope and their crews included four RAF specialists each, who were responsible for handling the balloons. In the summer of 1940 another barrage balloon squadron was formed and a 20th Control Centre was organised at Lyness. It could operate up to 56 balloons, but due to weather conditions, it was considered a significant success to keep 40 balloons in the air at once. In January 1941, in connection with the further increase in the number of balloons, another reorganisation was carried out, which resulted in formation of 950 Balloon Squadron AAF, that comprised all the balloons. It was the largest British unit of its kind with 62 positions on land (19 on Hoy, 9 on South Walls, 19 on Flotta Island, 6 on Fara Island, 2 on Cava Island and 1 on Rysa Island). Each position had its own electric winch with additional equipment. Roads were also built, leading to each of them. Moreover, there were 19 drifters adapted for towing balloons.

It was not easy to keep the barrage balloons in combat readiness. The fact that during the winter of 1943–1944 alone, 350 balloons were lost due to damage or by being ripped from their tethers, including 39 that were lost one day during a particularly violent squall, shows the scale of the problems. The Women's Auxiliary Air Force was responsible for making repairs (patching) to the balloons. It was a very hard and thankless work. There were also periodic problems with balloon gas. There were no hydrogen plants in Orkney and the entire demand was covered by supplies from Leith and Aberdeen.

During the war the construction of such a plant began, but production had not started before May 1945. The mobile hydrogen generators installed on trucks, which had been brought from the mainland, were unable to cover all the needs. Barrage balloons remained at Scapa Flow until June 1944. At that time, the threat of enemy air raids against the anchorage was rapidly minimised, while the demand for that kind of equipment in London rapidly increased, since the capital was being bombarded by V-1 flying bombs. Therefore, the entire 950 Balloon Squadron was embarked on two Liberty class ships and redeployed to the mainland.

Setting up of an auxiliary unit barrage balloon. (http://www.bbrclub.org)

A 94 mm anti-aircraft gun used by the 226th Battery. (K. Kubiak)

Stone mooring anchor used for mooring barrage balloons in vicinity of the Fleet Air Arm base HMS Sparrowhawk. (www.gramho.com)

Barrage balloon repair centre on the Island of Hoy as seen from Wee Fea in 1943. (NA, ref. ADM116/5790)

A Fordson E817T truck used for handling barrage balloons. It had two eight-cylinder engines of 30 hp each, one powered the car and the other a winch with 2,130 m of 7.9 mm cable. Collection of the RAF Museum, Hendon. (K. Kubiak)

The Air Force

Following the German occupation of Norway, the threat to the anchorage increased not only from motor torpedo boats but also, and perhaps even more so, from the enemy air force. The *Luftwaffe* raids on Scapa Flow, in which the enemy suffered minimal losses, made it clear to the British command that there was a need to strengthen the fighter contingent stationed in the Orkney Islands. That was absolutely essential if Scapa Flow was to become a well defended naval base. Despite a shortage of fighter units, 43, 111 and 605 Squadrons RAF (two flying Hurricanes, one using Gladiators) were redeployed to the Wick airbase. Additional, the newly formed 840 Squadron (flying Gloster Gladiator biplanes) was also redeployed to Orkney with the help of the navy. It was stationed at Hatston, which previously served as the base of 771 Fleet Air Arm Squadron. During the Norwegian campaign twin-engine Bristol Blenheims, used as long-range fighters, also operated from Hatston.

An important step to improve the air defences was the establishment of a joint command post responsible for anti-aircraft artillery and fighter aircraft units. That allowed for the most rational utilisation of the forces and resources the British had at their disposal.

The Hatston Fleet Air Arm base (HMS *Sparrowhawk*), as already mentioned, was flying Supermarine Walrus flying boats and Gloster Gladiator fighters organised into two squadrons. It was later flying

Fairey Swordfish aircraft taxiing on the runway of the Naval Air Station Hatston, aka HMS Sparrowhawk. (Public domain)

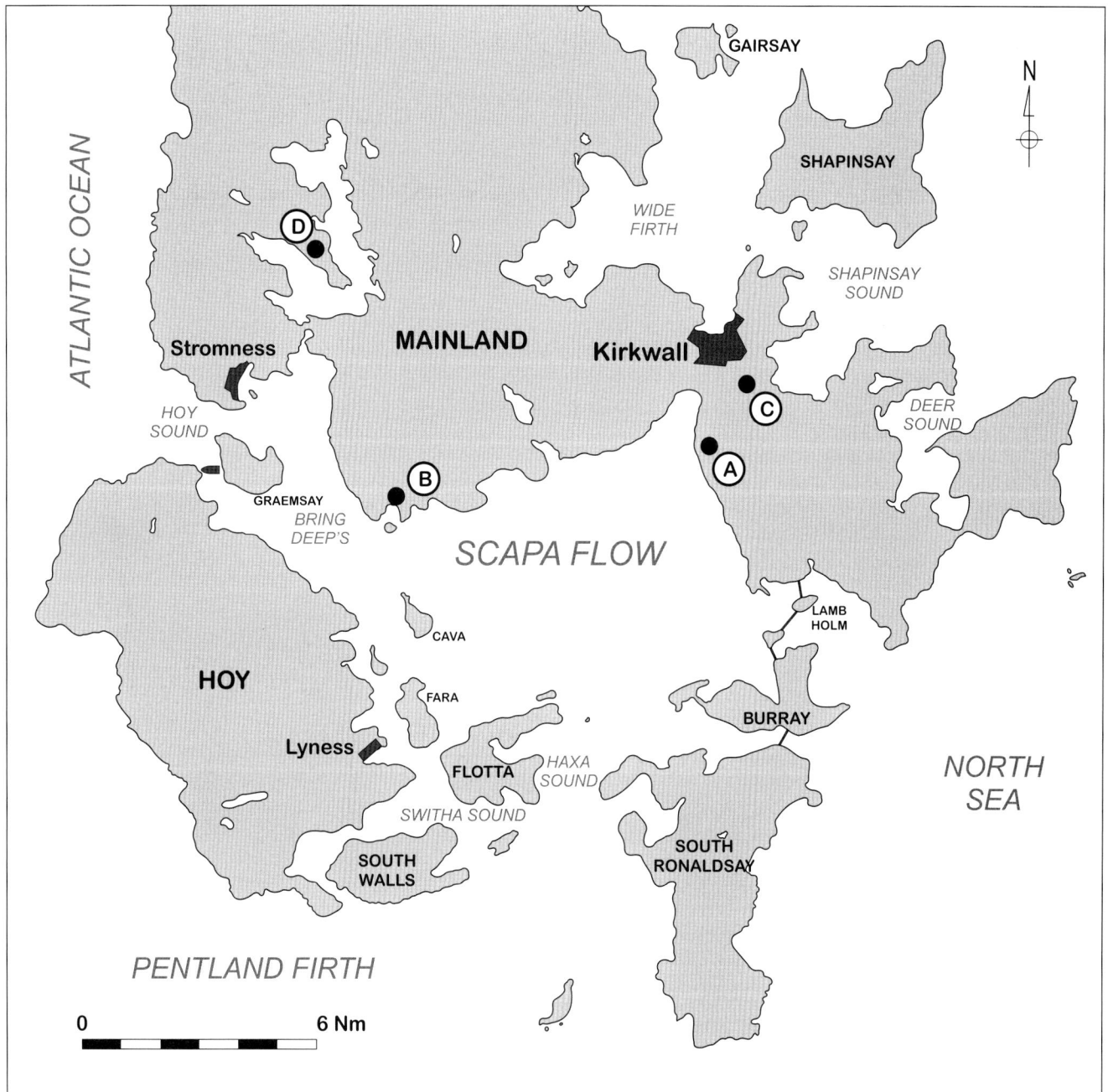

Air force bases in Orkney
during World War II.
A. HMS Robin (Grimsetter),
B. HMS Sparrowhawk
(Hatston),
C. HMS Tern (Twatt),
D. RAF Skeabrae.

Blackburn Skua fighter bombers, Fairey Swordfish torpedo bombers and even Bristol Blenheim light bombers, the latter not part of the Fleet Air Arm but from the RAF. In the spring and summer of 1941, RAF Martin Maryland reconnaissance aircraft of 771 Naval Air Squadron were based there for some time due to their involvement in the operation against the *Bismarck*.

In the later period, Hatston became an important training base. Taking advantage of the fact that threat posed by enemy activity was relatively low there (although it existed nevertheless), the FAA conducted the final stage of squadron operational training there before sending aircrew into action. From the end of 1941, the base was also used by US forces. It was at this time that a US Navy task force arrived at Scapa Flow, which comprised the battleship USS *Washington*, two heavy cruisers, six destroyers and the aircraft carrier USS *Wasp*. The latter brought to Orkney three squadrons of Vought SB2U Vindicator dive bombers. Their pilots underwent five-week-long training there. British aircraft were redeployed to Twatt airfield (HMS *Tern*) in the western part of Mainland. At the end of the training cycle, the US task force set off for the Mediterranean Sea, to participate in an operation aimed at delivering supplies to Malta.

The Americans returned to Orkney in the autumn of 1943, when the aircraft carrier USS *Ranger* dropped anchor at Scapa Flow. Her carrier-based squadrons passed through a training cycle and participated in operations against enemy shipping off the coast of Norway. In total, more than 200 British and American squadrons benefited from the use of HMS *Sparrowhawk* as a training centre during the war. The last squadron trained in the Orkney Islands during the war was an experimental unit flying Sikor-

sky R-4 Hoverfly helicopters. It could even be argued that the presence of 719 Squadron was symbolic. It ended one era and ushered in another in the history of naval aviation.

Hatston was undoubtedly the largest and best developed military aviation facility in the Orkney Islands. Therefore, after the war, it was taken over by the local authorities and transformed into a temporary airport.

In addition to HMS *Sparrowhawk*, there were three more Royal Air Force and Fleet Air Arm bases in the Orkney Islands during the war. The Fleet Air Arm originally operated from Twatt and Skeabrae, while the Royal Air Force used Grimsetter, located east of Kirkwall. However, eventually the RAF took control of Skeabrae, and naval aviation was deployed at Grimsetter, which was dubbed HMS *Robin*.

Construction work on Twatt air force base (dubbed HMS *Tern*) started in June 1940. It was mainly carried out by Royal Marine Engineers. The first group of naval aviation personnel arrived there in March 1941. The base served as a secondary airfield for HMS *Sparrowhawk*. Between June 1941 and March 1942, 809, 812, 819, 821 and 880 Squadrons, undergoing advanced training, were based there. It was there where the British aircraft were redeployed while the Americans were being trained. At a later date, another four British squadrons underwent intensive training there, as preparation for "Operation Torch" (the landing in North Africa). Another "hot" period for the Twatt base was an over year-long preparation cycle for the Fleet Air Arm forces that would participate in the invasion of the continent. At that time, HMS *Tern* was receiving squadrons flying, among others, the Supermarine Seafire, Hawker Sea Hurricane and Fairey Fulmar. The last Fleet Air Arm units stationed in Orkney were 802 and 771 Squadrons, withdrawn in July 1945. The growing importance of HMS *Tern* was indicated by the increase in the number of motor vehicles in service. In 1941, these included a motorbike, a 3-ton truck, a fire engine and an ambulance, while in 1944 there were 103 vehicles of different types.

For some time Twatt airfield was treated as a military backup installation. However, when it became apparent that Hatston did not work as a civilian airport (due to its location in relation to Kirkwall), the local authorities took an interest in the facility and over time took it over. Nowadays, having been expanded and modernised, the former Fleet Air Arm base HMS *Tern* is the islands' main airport.

The construction of the Skeabrae base (which the Fleet Air Arm planned would be another "satellite" airfield of the Hatston base), adjacent to Twatt, started in the spring of 1940. In May of the same year, still far from completion, the base was handed over to the RAF. That was due to the intention to

United States Secretary of the Navy Frank Knox during his visit aboard the aircraft carrier Ranger CV-4, *based at Scapa Flow, September 1943. (U.S. Naval History and Heritage Command, NH 70079).*

47

Warehouse that stored the equipment of the Battery Skerry Graemsay on Hoy armed with two 76.2 mm guns. (K. Kubiak)

deploy a dedicated fighter aircraft force on the islands following the German air raids on Scapa Flow. The first members of the aviation staff arrived at the base in August and what they saw could be described as lunar landscape. Despite intensification of the construction work, the first Hurricanes of the three fighter squadrons assigned to Orkney landed at their new airport in January 1941. The fighters had relatively few opportunities to fight enemy aircraft over the islands themselves, but they flew offensive hunting patrols and mainly engaged German long-range Condor bombers.

Occasionally, fighter units flying Spitfires were stationed at Skeabrae. In February 1944 two planes of 602 Squadron, transferred to Orkney "to rest", shot down a German Messerschmitt Bf 109G fighter, about 50 nautical miles from the islands. Since the British fighters were Mk.VIIs adapted for high-altitude flights, the enemy fighter was intercepted at an altitude of 12,000 metres.

In October 1944, the RAF's 611 Squadron based at Skeabrae scored two victories. First, a Ju 88 conducting photographic reconnaissance over Scapa Flow was intercepted and shot down, and then another machine of the same type was downed by a fighter escorting bombers flying a mission against coastal targets in Norway.

In January 1945, the first Canadian squadron arrived at the base, since its personnel had been withdrawn from the western front to rest. The base was used until September 1945, when the last unit stationed there, 451 Squadron RAF, departed.

Grimsetter started its service as an operational base in October 1940. At that time it was the so-called Fighter Sector Station for No. 14 Group RAF, used together with Skaebrae airfield. From June 1942, 132 Squadron flying Supermarine Spitfire fighters was stationed there, replaced in the spring of the following year by 129 Squadron using the same aircraft.

In June 1943, the base was taken over by the Fleet Air Arm, and dubbed HMS *Robin*. Like Hatston, Grimsetter became an important training centre. Squadrons flying Fairey Firefly, Grumman Avenger, Vought Corsair, Grumman Hellcat, Grumman Wildcat and other aircraft underwent advanced training there. The first unit trained there was a squadron which comprised 12 Grumman Tarpon planes (British designation of the American Grumman TBF Avenger), disembarked from the escort aircraft carrier HMS *Ravager*. By the end of the war, a full training cycle was completed by 20 Fleet Air Arm squadrons.

One of the auxiliary vessels used in northern Scotland and in the Orkney Islands by the Royal Air Force. (RAF Museum, Hendon)

Scapa Flow in April 1942. The U.S. aircraft carrier Wasp *can be seen in the fore-ground, with the battleship* Washington, *heavy cruiser* Wichita *and the British aircraft carrier (probably the* Illustrious) *and the battleship* King George V *in the background (U.S. Naval History and Heritage Command, NH 11925).*

Anti-landing defences

The campaign in the west, especially the successes of the German paratroopers in Belgium and the Netherlands, forced the strengthening of the anti-landing defences at Scapa Flow. As the British could not afford to deploy their line troops in the Orkney Islands (every battalion was of value at that time), it was decided to expand the tasks of anti-aircraft and coastal artillery. With the help of civilian workers, the artillerymen began to work on the expansion of field fortifications. They were additional equipped with small arms and machine guns and the stockpile of firearms ammunition were increased. The 94 mm and 40 mm anti-aircraft gun emplacements were rebuilt so that the guns could be quickly rolled out and used to fight ground targets. Up to the position of the infantry detachment, the logistics service was equipped with small arms. The culmination of all these undertakings was strenuous basic military training for all forces in the Orkney garrison.

At that time, prefabricated combat shelters erected near important buildings, on beaches considered convenient locations for enemy landing and potential paratrooper drop areas, became a characteristic

Soldiers of the Gordon Highlanders during an anti-landing exercise in the Orkney Islands. (NA, ref. WO166/12598)

feature of the islands' landscape. In several locations square-pyramidal reinforced concrete fortifications, meant to impede the movement of armoured vehicles and called "dragon's teeth", were laid.

In May 1940, the British government decided to establish a national voluntary paramilitary formation for territorial defence. It was originally named Local Defence Volunteers but was soon renamed the Home Guard. Within 24 hours of Prime Minister Eden's dedicated radio speech, 50 islanders volunteered. A week later, there were 200 volunteers. Most of them were veterans of the Great War, often with considerable experience. However, there were also veterans of the Victorian period wars. They were no longer capable of line duty, but by defending their homes they could have unexpectedly proved to be a tough opponent. A large portion of the volunteers came with their own hunting weapons, as the Home Guard had many more volunteers than rifles (at the beginning of July, there were only 490 rifles and 25,000 pieces of ammunition available for 529 volunteers). In a short period of time a system of observation points was organised and a communications network was developed to allow for the volunteers to be immediately called to arms. Eventually, the Orkney Home Guard was expanded into two battalions and several independent companies located on the northern islands. There were no Home Guard sub-units on Papay, North Ronaldsay and Graemsay only because of the small populations.

The Home Guard may have been a valuable element of local defence, but it could not be used as a manoeuvring force. Two companies of the 61st and 62nd Searchlight Regiments and a company of the 7th Gordon Highlanders stationed in Kirkwall and a company issued by the 435th Searchlight Battery and the 908th Service Company located in Kirkwall were assigned to this task. The defence system had shown great flexibility and fast response times during the false alarm caused by the Netherbutton radar operator's report claiming the detection of 150 enemy aircraft. The headquarters, expecting an air landing, put all its forces on alert. Although it finally turned out that the report was caused by equipment malfunction, the whole incident was a valuable test of the functionality of the systems adopted during the creation of the Orkney land defence system.

A Bren Carrier used by a British unit stationed in Orkney during World War II. (K. Kubiak)

The Fleet returns to Scapa Flow

The warships and auxiliary units entering Scapa Flow were preceded by a truly unusual vessel, one of the so-called "Winston's phantoms". She was the large, thirty-year-old steamer *Waimana*, disguised to look like the battleship *Resolution*. The creation of a mock-up flotilla posing as capital ship, another one of Churchill's ideas, was to hide the weak numbers of the Royal Navy, hamper the enemy's ability to find the real location of the most important British warships, create chaos within the German reconnaissance system and undermine commanders' trust towards information obtained via this channel. At a later time, Scapa Flow was entered by the "double" of the aircraft carrier HMS *Hermes*, built on the hull of the ship *Mamari*.

Foredeck of the Nelson *or the* Rodney. *A Town class cruiser can be seen in the background. Early camouflage scheme and additional equipment aboard the battleship suggest that the photo was taken upon return of the Home Fleet to Scapa Flow, which began on March 12, 1940. Following the sinking of the* Royal Oak, *the main force of the navy was withdrawn to Scotland until the anti-aircraft defences of Orkney could be strengthened. (A. Jarski's collection)*

Commander-in-Chief Home Fleet (1939–1940), Admiral Charles Morton Forbes. (Public domain)

At the beginning of March, a group of auxiliary ships concentrated at the Scapa Flow anchorage in order to protect fleet operations. It comprised the victuals depot ship *Boniface*, the *Voltaire* which stored dry goods and the accommodation ship *Dunluce Castle*. The latter was fitted with dentist offices and a cinema-theatre hall with 250 seats. It was also a centre for military mail and the navy photographic services.

On March 12, five days after the initially planned date, the Home Fleet entered Scapa Flow again. Winston Churchill, who wanted to witness the moment, boarded Admiral Forbes's flagship, HMS *Nelson*, at the Clyde. However, the passing of the fleet, at that time comprising five battleships and battlecruisers, a squadron of cruisers and a flotilla of destroyers, was not without incident. Prior to entering Hoxa Sound, Admiral Forbes received a signal informing him of German aircraft detected over the anchorage. That could have indicated enemy mine laying operations. In those circumstances, the fleet was halted until the entrance to the strait had been swept for mines. Churchill was not willing to wait and was transported to Scapa Flow aboard a destroyer that moved through Switha Sound. The First Lord of the Admiralty was visibly moved by the situation and, with incredible dramatic tension, cited Kipling's poem "Mine Sweepers" to the ship's commanding officer.

Several days later, the base's reinforced defence system was tested in combat. On March 8, three Junkers 88 aircraft, flying a routine reconnaissance mission over the Orkney Islands, spotted the well

Crew of a 76 mm gun aboard a drifter on a patrol duty in Scapa Flow. (IWM A 17176)

A 40 mm Bofors gun in a battery near Stromness. (IWM, H 39439).

known *Iron Duke*, auxiliary units and a capital ship (a decoy ship) in the base. This was a prelude to an attack on March 16. Eighteen Junkers Ju 88 aircraft of KG 30 attacked the ships and the base at Scapa Flow. Sixteen Heinkel He 111 bombers of KG 26 attacked the Fleet Naval Arm station HMS *Sparrow-hawk* at Hatston. The Germans heavily damaged the heavy cruiser HMS *Norfolk*, killing nine men, and scored another hit on the *Iron Duke*. However, they were unable to inflict substantial damage within the airfield infrastructure or among the aircraft on the ground. Instead, the bombs fell on the village of Brig O'Waithe.

The British anti-aircraft defence was not caught by surprise. Although the radar station at Nether-button did not detect the enemy aircraft approaching at low altitude, the radar station on the Shetland Islands reported "bandits" at 19.33, 14 minutes prior to the attack. The raid was met with fire from 52 heavy (of 68 mounted) and 17 (of a total of 28) lightweight anti-aircraft guns. However, no hits were scored despite 30 lights searching the skies. Fighter aircraft were not scrambled. To solve the problem of early enemy detection General Kemp suggested deploying a ship equipped with modern radar systems to Scapa Flow. The ship would act as radar surveillance unit and remain at Netherbutton until the station's radar was replaced with a more modern device.

However, that was a thing of the future. To immediately increase the effectiveness of anti-aircraft fire, the defences had to be reorganised. So far, without radar gun layers, each battery or gun squad fired individually after detecting targets visually. The new solution was to deploy all guns to create a barrage of fire for three minutes in the general direction of a predicted enemy aircraft attack, and after that provide aimed fire.

The barrage fire was tested on April 2, when Scapa Flow was attacked by 12 bombers. As the threat had been detected, all batteries were manned. Although the anti-aircraft guns scored no hits, their fire prevented the enemy from conducting effective attacks. The Germans retreated with one aircraft (a Heinkel He 111) heavily damaged by machine gun fire from the Ness battery.

At the beginning of 1940, Scapa Flow was the place of concentration for groups detached for "Operation Wilfred" – laying mine barrages in coastal shipping lanes along the Scandinavian peninsula.

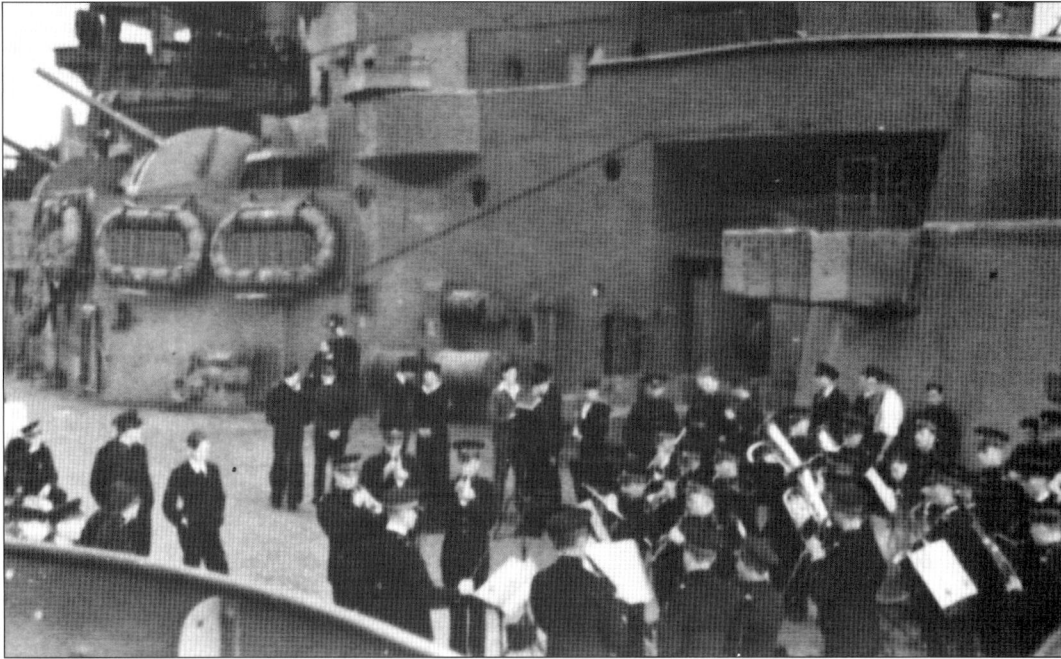

Its aim was to disrupt German shipments of ore from the Swedish Kiruna mine transported via the non-freezing harbour of Narvik. The so-called WS Force comprised the minelayer *Teviotdale* and four destroyers. The group's task was to lay a mine barrage in the area of Stradlandet. "Operation Wilfred" was initially planned for May 5 and later postponed to May 8, but three WS Force groups left Scapa Flow according to the initial schedule. Two other mine groups had a total of 10 destroyers (including four carrying mines) with operational cover provided by the battlecruiser HMS *Renown* with an escort of four destroyers.

At that time the Orkney base was also home to a task force which was to be deployed as the escort for landing forces of "Operation R4" to seize the Norwegian harbours of Stavanger, Bergen, Trondheim and Narvik. The task force comprised the battleships HMS *Rodney* and *Valiant*, the battlecruiser HMS *Repulse*, the light cruisers HMS *Sheffield* and *Penelope* and ten destroyers, supported by the French light cruiser *Emile Bertin* accompanied by two destroyers. The landing forces were concentrated at Rosyth and Clyde.

In the evening of April 8, the German air force, taking advantage of the high number of ships concentrated at Scapa Flow, attacked the anchorage. This time the attackers had been detected 80 nautical

miles from the islands by the aerial surveillance radar of the cruiser HMS *Curlew* deployed to the Orkney Islands (according to General Kemps' suggestion) as a radar surveillance ship.

Not only had all batteries been manned but also the RAF fighters of Wick were scrambled. Around 24 to 30 aircraft participated in the attack (publications provide different information on that matter). The attackers were met with barrage fire which forced their crews to release their payload from high altitudes, which greatly reduced accuracy. The British claimed three enemy aircraft destroyed by ground fire (a fourth Heinkel 111 bomber emergency landed at Wick airfield with two crewmen killed and a wounded pilot) and three more shot down by the fighters from Wick. Several German airmen bailed out, two of them were rescued from water on the coast at Burray, the others probably perished at sea. This may be deduced by the fact that an empty dinghy was found in the area of Fair Isle. The prisoners later testified that the target of the attack was to be Lyness and the boom defences at Hoxa Sound. The airmen were surprised by the density of the anti-aircraft fire, which made effective bombing impossible.

The attack on April 8 was strictly connected to the initiation of the Norwegian Campaign. Scapa Flow's importance increased and in a matter of hours the anchorage became the "front base", located only 300 nautical miles from the coast of the Scandinavian peninsula. Despite most of the *Luftwaffe* forces being involved in direct support operations for the ground troops and engaging British forces in Norwegian waters, harassing attacks against Scapa Flow did not stop. On the evening of April 9 the radar of HMS *Curlew* detected groups of approaching enemy aircraft. Initial estimates, based on the radar reading, stated the number of aircraft to be about 60, however, it turned out that only about 20 He 111s and Ju 88s participated in the attack. The Germans again concentrated on attacking Lyness and the boom defences but were unable to break them. The attacks were repulsed not only by the anti-aircraft artillery but also by crews of the coastal artillery firing their machine guns and the ships in the base. The heavy cruiser HMS *Suffolk* sustained minor damage from German bombs (there were no human losses and the ship was able to remain in service). Two men were killed on land and one of the coastal guns at South Rolandsay sustained minor damage. In comparison, German losses were very high. Three planes were shot down by the anti-aircraft artillery, two more by Hurricanes that had been scrambled from Wick. At least four more aircraft were damaged. The aerial defences of Scapa Flow again proved their worth.

The German involvement in operations in Norway meant the *Luftwaffe* had no means to attack the Orkney Islands during the next couple of days. On April 24, five enemy aircraft appeared over the island, this time approaching from the west. The Germans attacked after dark, at about 10pm, which along

The German light cruiser Königsberg. She took part in the invasion of Norway, assign to carry troops to Bergen. On April 9, she was hit three times by 210 mm coastal battery guns at Kvarven Fort and remained in the Norwegian harbour, while the remaining German warships returned to home waters. On April 10, she was attacked by 16 Blackburn Skua aircraft of 800 and 803 Naval Air Squadrons, operating from RNAS Hatston in the Orkney Islands. Five 500-pound bombs decided the cruiser's fate. Eighteen crew member perished with the ship.

with bad weather conditions made target identification impossible. As a result, the enemy bombed wrecks sunk at Holm Sound and hills on the island of Hoy, where there were no military installations. The attackers suffered no losses.

After the defence systems, especially the anti-aircraft defences, had been improved, Scapa Flow became a real haven for the fleet. In the following months, German air force operations were limited to reconnaissance missions, the base itself was not attacked by large forces. It allowed the saving of several ships damaged during operations in Norwegian waters and in the North Sea. One of them was the heavy cruiser HMS *Suffolk*, bombed at Stavanger.

The British naval air forces also conducted offensive operations by aircraft based at Scapa Flow. From April to October, three FAA squadrons (800, 801, and 803) were transferred to Hatston and equipped with the Blackburn Skua aircraft. They would attack German shipping on the Norwegian coast. The aircraft operated in groups from two to twenty machines each. Their biggest success came at the very beginning, on April 10, 1940. The British aircraft took off only 12 hours after a large *Luftwaffe* air strike against the Orkney Islands. Sixteen Skua aircraft left Hatston (seven of 800 and nine from 803 Squadron). Each of them was armed with a 226 kg armour-piercing demolition bomb. After two hours of flight, the attackers crossed the Norwegian coast line and began their approach towards Bergen. The German cruiser *Königsberg* was detected in the harbour. The British began their dive bombing attack from about 2,700 metres and, despite heavy anti-aircraft fire, scored three hits on the ship's hull. Fires that broke out on the cruiser could not be contained and as a result *Königsberg* capsized and sank. Fifteen planes returned to base, only one of the Skuas was lost, killing the leader of 803 Squadron's third section, Lt. Bryan John Smeeton, and his crewman Mid. (A) Fred Watkinson.

An attempt to repeat the successful mission failed. On October 1, Fairey Swordfish biplane torpedo bombers attacked the battleship *Scharnhorst* returning south. The attack resulted in the loss of two aircraft.

Blackburn Skua dive bomber/fighter aircraft. These aircraft, operating with squadrons based in Orkney, sank the German light cruiser Königsberg *in Bergen harbour.*

The following months were relatively calm. Harassing attacks by the German air force caused minor damage. During a raid on July 16 and another one at night from July 20 to 21 only one person was lightly wounded. A night raid on June 2/3 also caused only minor damage.

On the night of August 27, 1940, the German air force conducted their first mine laying operation. Five aircraft dropped parachute mines in the area of the island of Burray and Water Sound. One of the mines was dropped on land and exploded near the Ladywater farm. On the following night the mine laying operation continued. It was conducted by single aircraft approaching at about 5 mile intervals towards the western exit of Hoy Sound. The mine laying missions were not intensive and the minesweepers easily managed to eliminate the threat. Single mines were destroyed with no losses. Lack of success of the German operation had two reasons, a serious operational error and technical imperfections of the mines. Operationally, one of the most important rules of naval mine warfare was broken – mines were to be deployed en masse. The technical problem was within the mine itself – the *Luftwaffe* used mines with parachutes, which enabled spotters to pinpoint the location of the devices.

Harassing and reconnaissance operations were continued. They did not pose a serious threat to the base or the ships, but they forced a high level of combat readiness to be maintained for a long time. A change in the combat routine of the anti-aircraft artillery and the Home Guard came on Christmas Day. A German reconnaissance plane was trying to assess the progress of work on the new naval air base at Skeabrea. Unexpectedly, the Ju 88 flew 200 metres over Stromness and headed for its target. Unfortunately for its crew, a Grumman Martlet (British designation for the American Grumman Wildcat fighter plane) had just landed at Skeabrea. Its pilot took off, chased the enemy reconnaissance plane and shot

The Fairey Swordfish, along with the Blackburn Skua, were the basic British Fleet Air Arm aircraft in the initial period of the war. The Skua had already been withdrawn from front line service in mid 1940, while Swordfish served in the European theatre until the end of hostilities.

The oldest of the British aircraft carriers, HMS Furious. The ship had departed Scapa Flow only 24 hours before Prien forced his way into the Orkney anchorage.

it down in the area of Loch of Skail. The German plane turned over while attempting to perform an emergency landing. Its crew emerged unscathed from the accident and attempted to set the aircraft on fire. Their attempt was thwarted by two members of the Home Guard who took the airmen prisoners.

Three weeks after the Christmas victory over the Ju 88, RAF fighters took off from Sumburgh on the Shetland Islands, intercepted and destroyed another enemy reconnaissance aircraft in the area of Fair Isle. This time the British scored a kill on a Heinkel 111. Further reconnaissance flights over the Orkney Islands meant that the German command was still interested in Scapa Flow.

At the beginning of 1941, the British began to build two new radar stations that would cover the "dead" sectors of the Netherbutton station. The radars were planned to be located on the island of South Walls neighbouring Mainland, and on the easternmost tip of the isle of Sanday. On March 8, 1941, the latter was targeted by a single Ju 88 aircraft. The German plane dropped two bombs and then strafed the buildings. At that time, there was no anti-aircraft artillery and British fighters were unable to intercept the enemy aircraft.

German pilots felt the threat of the anti-aircraft defences deployed around Scapa Flow and, for their attacks against the Orkney Islands, they chose targets located on the outer islands, in many cases with no military value. In March, the enemy attacked a lighthouse at Auskerry. In May, two bombs fell on the island of Flotta. It seems that the British themselves, presented the enemy with the location of their important installations. Despite the low cover of clouds, the altitude of barrage balloons was not decreased. As a result, they were clearly seen above the clouds giving the bomber aircraft crews a perfect hint.

The German air force also attacked Allied shipping west of the Orkney Islands. Aircraft taking off from bases in Norway usually entered the Atlantic via the Fair Isle Gap and returned through the Pentland Firth. When approaching their area of operation, the pilots tried to maintain a low altitude in order to avoid detection by radar stations on the Shetlands and Orkneys. In that case, even when the British aircraft were airborne, their pilots had to detect the enemy visually with no guidance from the ground. In the following months the *Luftwaffe* continued reconnaissance missions over Scapa Flow, however bombing raids with large numbers of aircraft did not take place.

At that time, the anti-aircraft defences at Scapa Flow were reinforced by 147th Battery equipped with a new weapon. These were unguided rocket-propelled missiles fitted with a time fuse. They were fired in salvos towards enemy aircraft and would explode at a given altitude, creating a shrapnel barrage. The method was similar to that employed by the anti-aircraft guns, however the guns had a much higher rate of fire. The missile launchers took a lot of time to reload.

Rodney *or* Nelson *probably manoeuvring in Forth of Clyde. (A. Jarski's collection)*

For most of her wartime service the ORP Błyskawica operated out of Scapa Flow and northern Scottish harbours. The photo shows her on the waters of Firth of Forth. (A. Jarski's collection)

The experience of the Norwegian campaign, when Scapa Flow became a haven for ships damaged by the enemy air force, made the British develop the maintenance infrastructure on the Orkney Islands. The aim was to build a repair base able to provide overhaul work on ships the size of a destroyer and immediate maintenance of larger units.

The decisions made in the summer of 1940 resulted in arrival of the *Admiralty Floating Dock no. 12* – AFD 12 to Scapa Flow on August 16. It was able to receive ships of displacement up to 1,500 tons, which was the equivalent of the size of the Tribal class destroyers. Fate decided that it was a ship of that class, HMS *Bedouin*, that first used the dock at Scapa Flow. Another docked destroyer was HMS *Mendip* whose stern was damaged by an explosion of her own depth charge.

In December of 1940, a 30 ton floating dock arrived at Scapa Flow. These two platforms (supported by a smaller crane belonging to Metal Industries) and coastal workshops (also owned by MI) comprised a repair complex of high capacity. Until June 1945, when the dock began its journey to the Far East, it had been used to overhaul 345 escort ships. These were 263 British destroyers, 80 submarines, frigates, corvettes, drifters and a dozen or so Allied, American and Russian ships. Apart from that, several dozen other ships were repaired by the Scapa Flow workshops. The largest were the escort aircraft carriers HMS *Chaser*, overhauled after running aground in July 1943 and HMS *Nabob*, torpedoed in August 1944 (she underwent preservation work before leaving for a shipyard).

HMS Victorious. *Until mid 1944 the ship operated in the Atlantic, often calling at Scapa Flow.*

As mentioned before, the entire effort of repair work in Scapa Flow until mid 1940 was the responsibility of Metal Industries. The company used almost its entire pre-war fleet, the ships *Metinda*, *Bertha*, *Salvage King*, *Indefatigable*, *William H. Hastie* and several drifters assigned by the navy. Until the end of the war, the company conducted 18 rescue operations oriented towards keeping ships afloat (beginning with the bombed *Iron Duke*) and 18 operations concerning merchantmen and transports. What is interesting is that the highest amount of work was provided for the MI crews not by the enemy but by the fury of the Orkney weather. For instance, during a one stormy November night in 1940, nine merchantmen were washed ashore by the waves. A year later, in December 1941, stormy waves pushed ashore two navy cruisers, a tanker, a collier and a drifter along with two merchant ships. None of the damaged ships sank, thanks to immediate action coordinated by

XMAS Morin *was a herring drifter in peacetime. After being mobilized and assigned to Orkney she retained the Santa Claus cartoon on her smokestack.*

a brilliant expert, Thomas McKenzie (the former rescue chief of the Cox and MI was drafted in the rank of commodore).

Between 1939 and 1945 several smaller ships were lost in Scapa Flow waters due to accidents. One of them was the drifter *Imbat* that sank on February 4, 1941 after colliding with a ship whose name has been impossible to determine. The wreck of that small, 92-ton ship has been lying in Gutter Sound until today, only 300 metres east of Lyness Pier, 14 metres below the surface.

A British aircraft carrier, October 28, 1941, Scapa Flow, aerial photograph.

Churchill's barriers

Sinking of the *Royal Oak* was a massive humiliation for the Royal Navy. That was why the First Sea Lord, Winston Churchill, was ready to undertake any actions to prevent similar events from happening again. Several days after the disaster, Churchill, participating in a session of the investigative committee studying the circumstances of losing the battleship, ordered the closing of the eastern straits. However, final decisions concerning construction of a barrier had not been made until March 1940.

It is worth noting that the idea of constructing a fixed barrier to secure the anchorage, not only against submarines but also light surface ships (torpedo boats, motor torpedo boats), had appeared at least twenty years earlier. In 1915 the Admiralty sent engineer William Halcrow to the Orkney Islands with the task of assessing the feasibility of such an undertaking. His assessment was moderately optimistic. He stated that the construction of the barrier was possible, however it would have required engaging huge resources for at least 18 months. The naval command did not accept the idea of closing the straits permanently.

During World War II, the Admiralty and its chief were determined to begin the enterprise and finish it whatever the cost. Initial studies began in 1940. In the early spring the hydrographic ship *Franklin*

Holm Sound before being closed by the "Churchill barrier". Line of wrecks, which were supposed to block the access to the anchorage, is clearly visible. (Orkney Library and Archive)

N

ORKNEY
MAINLAND

Moss Quarry

Bossack Blockyard

Bossack Blockyard

Headquarters
of Balfour
Beatty

St. Mary's

Rockworks Blockyard

St. Mary's Wharf

1 KIRK SOUND

SCAPA FLOW

Lamb Holm Blockyard

Camp 60 and an Italian Chapel

Lamb Holm Wharf

2

Lamb Holm Quarry

Glimps Holm Wharf

SKERRY SOUND

Glimps Holm Quarry

EAST WEDDEL SOUND

3

Links Quarry

Warebanks Blockyard
Camp 34

Warebanks Quarry

ECHNALOCH BAY

Echna
Loch

BURRAY

Housebreck Quarry

Burray Wharf

4

South Burray Blockyard

Ayre of Cara

WATER SOUND

Hoxa Quarry

SOUTH RONALDSAY

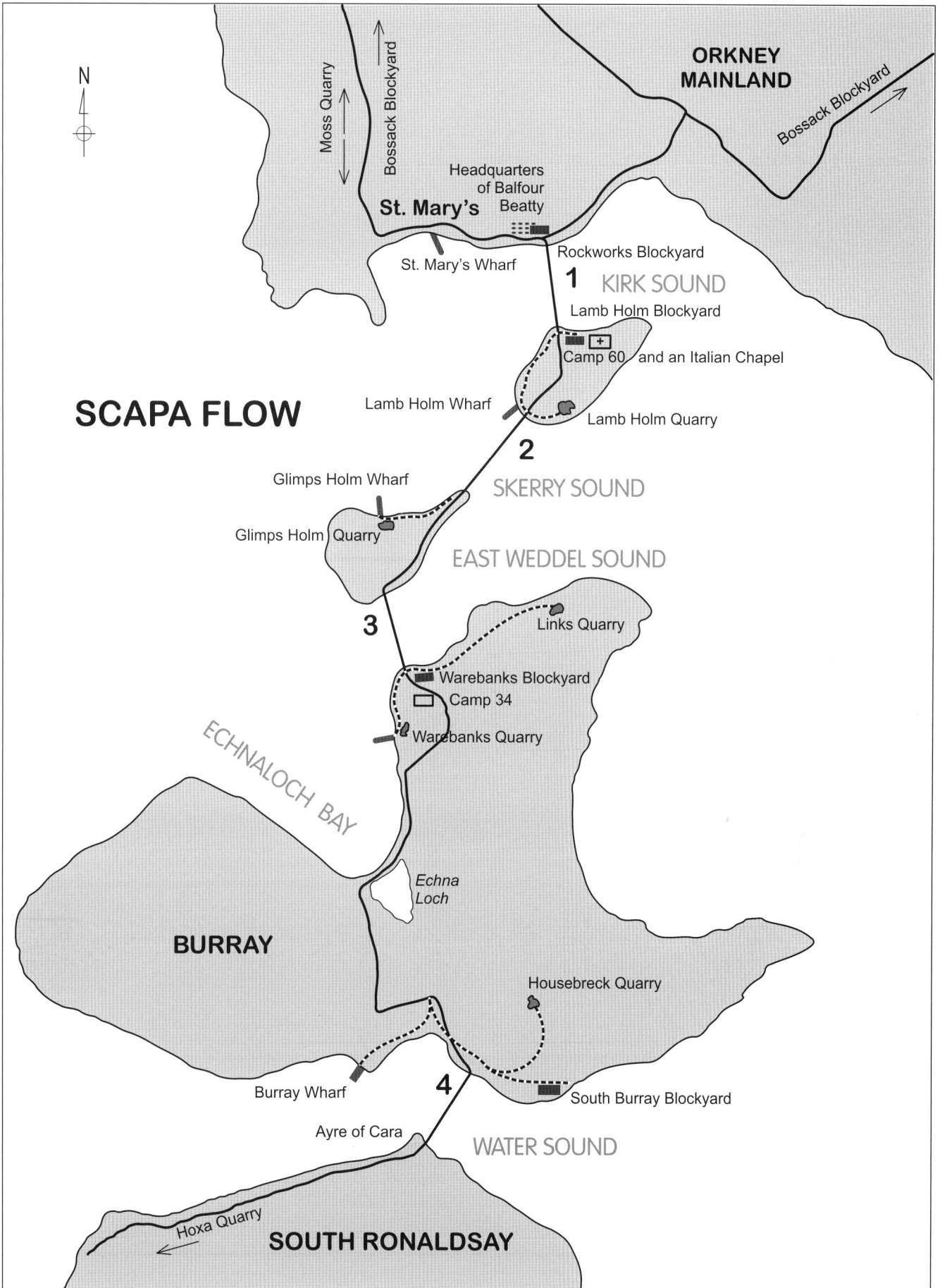

1, 2, 3 and 4 with the basic building infrastructure. The location of the Italian POW camp and the Italian Chapel are marked.

conducted detailed reconnaissance of the eastern straits, making thousands of measurements of depths, directions and speeds of tidal currents. Based on the documentation, Professor Gibson of Leeds University made models of the straits that would be used to create the most optimal engineering solutions. Studying models prior to designing hydrotechnical structures was not popular at the time and Gibson was certainly the forerunner of the idea.

Simultaneously with design work, the Admiralty searched for a contractor for that complicated investment. The navy chose Balfour Beatty & Company Ltd that was involved in other work in the Orkney Islands. Managers of Balfour Beatty, having acquired the contract, would use their resources

The Italian Chapel at Camp 60, located near Kirk Sound. It was built by Italian prisoners of war, who were forced to help with the construction of the "Church-ill barriers". (K. Kubiak)

The interior of the Italian Chapel is a lamentation, longing and nostalgia of the southerners who found themselves under the north-ern sky. (K. Kubiak)

to probe the market for reliable subcontractors. The list of companies involved in hydrotechnical work was not very long. One of the first companies was that of John M. Henderson, which had participated in construction of the Kut El-Amara dam on the Tigris in Iraq. The company's transport park included cable transporters (a kind of cable railway) for lowering stone blocks directly to their destination along the barrier foundations.

The planned investment was a huge engineering and organizational challenge. For example, it meant accommodating large numbers of additional workers in the Orkney Islands. The problem was solved with the 26-year-old passenger ship *Almanzora* that was adapted as a floating warehouse and a base ship for the first phase of the enterprise. All necessary devices and materiel were loaded on the ship. In the Orkney Islands, 230 workers and a team of 20 engineers were accommodated on the ship. During summer, additional workers were housed in tents in camps at Lamb Holm and Glimps Holm. By September, complexes of barracks were constructed, Rockworks at Holm on the island of Lamb Holm and two more on the island of Burray.

According to the design, the barrier was to be constructed of stone blocks and breakstone flanked on both sides with concrete blocks. In order to strengthen the structure, breakstone was planned to be placed in special baskets called gabions, with edges configured in a way allowing them to be hooked to one another. A two-lane road was to run along the top of the construction. Initial specification estimated the required material at 580,000 tons of stone (and 66,000 baskets/gabions) and 333,000 tons of concrete. The cable transporters were crucial for the project. It had been estimated that, due to strong tidal currents, it was impossible to block the straits by building a dam starting from each of the opposite banks. That would cause waters to swell in the central section. The only solution was to evenly cover the entire width of the straits with stones and concrete block thrown into the water from the air via the cable transporters.

According to the project, the Orkney Islands themselves were to provide material to fill in the barriers. Blocks of specific shape and dimensions were to be cut out from the bedrock. That required work with use of explosives and pneumatic hammers. Tools powered by compressed air forced construction of a compressor station with its own electrical generators. To safely install the generators, the company had to construct buildings and the Admiralty was obligated to provide the necessary fuel.

The quarries were placed:
- on Mainland – Moss Quarry
- on Lamb Holm – Lamb Holm Quarry
- on Glimps Holm – Glimps Holm Quarry (abandoned due to poor quality of the mined material)
- on Burray – Links Quarry (northern shore), Warebanks Quarry (western shore), Housebreck Quarry (southern shore)
- on South Ronaldsay – Hoxa Quarry.

Concrete blocks were also to be cast locally, which determined the need for cement, sand, water, tools and, what was most important, transport. Every ton of concrete had to be transported by sea from Scotland and England as the Orkney Islands had no cement plant. The workshops casting concrete blocks were placed:
- on Mainland: near St Mary's Hope – Rockworks Blockyard (November 1942 – October 1944), near Tankerness (end of 1942) – Bossack Blockyard (July 1943 – January 1944)
- on Lamb Holm – Lamb Holm Blockyard (March 1943 – June 1944)
- on Burray: Warebanks Blockyard (northern shore, September 1942 – October 1944), South Burray Blockyard (southern shore, March 1943 – June 1944)
- on South Ronaldsay – Grimsetter Blockyard.

Apart from the latter workshop, closed at the beginning of 1943, the others kept production going until mid 1944. All workshops in total cast 34,385 five-ton blocks, 15,036 ten-ton blocks and 2,226 4.8-ton blocks. At the peak of their production, the workshops would pour concrete into 30 blocks an hour.

During the first stage of preparation work, the area for all necessary infrastructure was decided. The main working grounds were situated on Lamb Holm, Glimps Holm and Burray. In their close proximity there appeared sturdy quays necessary for unloading supplies and material transported by sea. Each of them had to withstand pressure exerted by a 10-ton self-propelled crane. The already existing quays on Holm and Burray were also employed. Each of the construction sites received its own electrical generator station. A total of five generator stations were constructed with the capacity of a small powerplant. They were built at:
- Lamb Holm – 2 x 325 kW
- Warebanks – 1 x 260 kW
- South Burray – 1x 260 kW
- St Mary's – 1 x 200 kW
- Grimsetter – 1 x 200 kW

The cruiser HMS Edin-burgh on the approaches to Scapa Flow. October 1941. (IWM, A 6160)

Rails were laid to connect the quarries with places where the cable transporters were to be installed. Steam engines and railway cars were also brought in. The range of the enterprise realised before proper work began was huge – about 1,000 workers were employed for a period of six months.

The next stage was the installation of the cable transporters. They were enormous, complex constructions that had to be anchored strongly into the ground. The first device was built at Weddel Sound, between the islands and Glimp Holm in June 1941.

At the end of 1941, the problem of a workforce deficit appeared. The British economy desperately needed qualified workers and a large number of men working on the barrier construction were sent south. The situation was solved by utilising Italian prisoners of war as forced labour. That, however, required special preparations. In October 1941, all work at the barriers was halted as all effort was put into construction of two prison camps. The first Italians, mostly carefully selected qualified workers, arrived at the Orkney Islands in January 1942. Initially the prisoners refused to work on the barriers claiming that they were *de facto* military installations (which was quite true at that time) and the Geneva Convention released them from the obligation of supporting military effort of their captors.

Finally, after talks between delegates of the British military administration and representatives of the prisoners, the Italians began their work. In March 1942, a double cable transporter was raised over Kirk Sound and in September a similar device was constructed over Skerry and Water Sound. At their disposal, the builders had five transporters including four electrically powered, brought from Iraq, and

Fuel pump of Lyness fuel depot. (K. Kubiak)

one steam powered, constructed to build a bridge over the Dornie River in Sutherland. The transporters spread over Kirk Sound had a span of 731 metres each, the device over Water Sound 777 metres and the transporter over Skerry Sound 752 metres. The transporters' masts were between 52 and 57 metres in height. The masts were connected by 635 mm diameter cables (each transporter had six of those) able to hold a mass of 10.75 tons. Their durability was calculated to withstand 125,000 such drops.

The order of work was as follows. First, two high bases of gabions were raised on the bottom, protected on both sides from being washed away by smaller layers of stone rubble. During the next stage of work, the space between the higher causeways was filled with loose stone rubble which made a base for a ridge of gabions. Then, the entire structure was covered with another layer of gabions filled with stone rubble and overlaid with concrete blocks. The heaviest elements were located at the foot of the structure. The last stage was to mould the top of the dyke and to build a road on top of the structure. However, this was possible only after the top of the causeway emerged from the surface of the water. The following table includes dates of reaching that stage.

DATES OF CLOSING THE EASTERN STRAITS WITH BARRIERS		
	Low tide	High tide
Kirk Sound	March 17, 1943	April 18,1943
Skerry Sound	April 21, 1943	June 4, 1943
East Weddel Sound	May 13, 1942	August 26, 1942
Water Sound	March 24, 1943	May 22, 1943

Therefore, it was not until three years after the sinking of the *Royal Oak* that the British managed to reliably close and secure the eastern straits against surface combatant and submarine incursions.

Construction of the barriers required employing numerous vessels, drifters, launches, scows and others. Their crews had to be aware of the fact that they were operating in extremely dangerous tidal waters. The scale of the dangers can be shown on the example of the drifter *Token*. While crossing Skerry Sound her screw was damaged and the drifting ship was immediately caught by tidal current which carried her towards Barrier No 2. The drifter was helped by the tugboat *Gabbeville* but the tow cable snapped when

Stone blocks forming the outer layer of Churchill's Barrier No. 4. (K. Kubiak)

67

The First Lord of Admirality, Albert Victor Alexander. He was in office three times, 1929–1931, 1940–1945, 1945–1946. (Public domain)

both ships were hit by a strong squall. Finally, the damaged ship ran aground on rocks on the shores of Glimpse Holm. The crew's fate seemed to have been sealed. However, the skipper of a small open boat, the *Kaki*, challenged fate and against all odds approached *Token*'s side and rescued her entire crew. The stormy waves and the fury of the tidal currents finished their destructive work in a relatively short time. After 48 hours the wreck of the wooden drifter disappeared, never to be seen again.

The steel barge *Dora* was also lost while being towed towards the Orkney Islands. She was crucial for the construction work but the vessel sank in the waters of Pentland Firth after a heavy storm hit the towing group.

After closing the approaches, a road was begun to be built atop the barrier. The construction work, of much less intensity, lasted for the entire year of 1944. Finally, the new but highly controversial "communication investment", as the "Churchill barriers" were named, was opened on May 12, 1945. The First Lord of the Admiralty, A. V. Alexander, was the guest of honour during the ceremony.

The "Churchill barriers" cost £2,500,000, including £750,000 spent on the transport park. Apart from the cable transporters discussed earlier, it included 24 cranes, 58 steam engines, 260 railway cars of different type, 19 excavators, 16 stone breakers, 51 lorries, 12 dump trucks. The work fleet included two steam tugboats, two drifters, a tanker, four liaison boats, a 350-ton hulk and 11 barges. Sixteen kilometres of railway line were laid during construction of the barriers.

The records above show enormous forces and resources engaged in the project. All that took place when Great Britain was suffering a huge deficit of workforce, steel, cement, vehicles, current generators and practically everything that was necessary to continue the military effort. Despite all this, such needed materials were not used to build fortifications on the eastern coast but to build barriers in the Orkney Islands. This was perhaps the most important result of Prien's raid, much more critical than sinking of the *Royal Oak*. As a result of the daring operation, the Royal Navy lost a ship but the British military economy was forced to devote several million work-days and thousands of tons of deficit material to construct security measures against another submarine, that would never arrive.

Nowadays, the "Churchill barriers" are a perfect, independent from weather conditions, connection between South Ronaldsay and Mainland, making the inhabitants of the south-west part of the archipelago the main beneficiaries of the entire investment. Such an undertaking would have not been conceivable in circumstances other than wartime. The small local community would have never been able to finance a communication lane between South Ronaldsay and Mainland.

On the other hand we have to remember that the barriers sealed the fate of fishermen living around Scapa Flow. The shortest way to the fishing grounds of the North Sea was this time definitely closed. That meant the end of the fishing industry.

An interesting and unusual memento was left in Orkney by the Italian workers. The prisoners of war, mostly Catholic, initially had limited possibilities to organise their spiritual life. The problem was solved after an agreement had been signed between the commandant of the prison camp No. 60, Major Buckland, and the POWs' chaplain, Giacobazzi. According to the agreement, the camp's authorities were to provide the Italians with two prefabricated concrete barracks in shape of a cylinder cut in half and materials for redecoration. In their free time the Italians were allowed to adapt the barracks for a chapel. The result exceeded all expectations. A group of prisoners working under the supervision of Domenico Chiocchetti created a work of art. The concrete barrack changed into a temple decorated with paintings that created the illusion of space. Additionally, the building received a concrete fronton built in the style of Italian chapels.

After the Italians had left, the chapel fell into decay. It was the only remnant of prison camp No. 60. The inhabitants of the Orkney Islands, who initially treated that wartime artefact with indifference, did not let the chapel become devastated. At the end of the 1950s, a communal committee was formed to renovate the unusual temple. With the help of the BBC they were able to find Chiocchetti who, at that time lived in Moena, a small village in the Dolomites. During the following years he visited the island several times to renew the painting in the chapel (he died in 1999 at the age of 89). The committee's activity did not end there. It has been active until today collecting means for preservation of the chapel and maintaining contact with former Italian prisoners and their families.

Wartime every-day reality

Between 1942 and 1943, the Orkney garrison had a total of 30,000 men. Apart from the military personnel, there were 3–4,000 civilian workers employed on the islands on the basis of the wartime work order. There were also several hundred Italian prisoners of war utilised for construction work. When we add the ships' crews, the military personnel made double the size of the permanent civilian population of the islands. Besides strengthening the defensive installations, there were also works concerning development of the logistics infrastructure that mostly concentrated in the area of the Lyness base.

By August 1942, the first underground fuel tanks were added. Norwegian miners, evacuated from Spitsbergen during the British raid on that island, contributed invaluably to the drilling work. By August 1943, the underground tanks reached their planned capacity of 100,000 tons. Apart from that, by November 1942 the entire infrastructure and fittings for effective refuelling of ships were built. There were three special piers (one concrete and two of metal) with fuelling stations. Fuel was transported with the use of steam pumps grouped in a freshly built pumping station. Besides fuel installations, Lyness also had storage of barrier nets and workshops for their maintenance and repair. They were placed in the area owned by the Metal Industries. At a distance from all devices, installations and barrack complexes there was a warehouse of underwater weapons with naval mines and torpedoes. Headquarters of the local navy command and a communication centre were built in 1942. To get the impression of the scale of all telephone communications, we should mention that the entire communication personnel at Scapa Flow in 1939 was 80 people while in 1944 the telephone exchange (8,800 calls a day) required 270 personnel (mostly from the Women's Royal Naval Service).

The increasing number of personnel caused temporary difficulties concerning accommodation, thus a huge effort was put into construction of barracks. In 1943 at Hoy there were already four navy barrack compounds, a separate compound for communication service members and an army barracks. They

LtCdr Romuald Nałęcz-Tymiński (Polish Navy), commanding officer of escort destroyer Ślązak. (Narodowe Archiwum Cyfrowe)

The escort destroyer ORP Ślązak at Scapa Flow, May 1942. (IWM, FL 789).

A group of British destroyers in the Orkney archipelago, shortly before or during the war, before the white quick identifications stripes on their funnels and turrets were removed. The Blanche *(hit a mine and sank on November 13, 1939) is in the foreground, the* Brilliant *is in the background. The photo may have been taken from the deck of the cruiser* Calypso, *which went down on June 12, 1940, south of Crete. (A. Jarski's collection)*

were able to house up to 15,000 people. According to British tradition, social and recreational facilities were built simultaneously. A military cinema began operating as early as 1940. In 1943, a new cinema hall was built, one of the biggest entertainment facilities in Europe. Close to one of the piers there was a Recreation Centre and the Naval Canteen with a military department store. It offered a full assortment of goods (in accordance with wartime regulations) including a wide range of spirits. This surprised the US Navy personnel, who took full advantage of the stocks as their service on US ships and bases was under full prohibition. One of the most important elements of the infrastructure were huge laundries that worked for the Scapa Flow personnel and the ships' crews.

Apart from investments at Lyness on Hoy, intensive work was in progress in other areas of the huge anchorage. New piers were constructed on the islands of Flotta and Calf of Flotta. St Margaret's Hope pier was enlarged to accommodate the drifters detached to tow barrage balloons.

At Hutton there was a special wooden pier designed for ferries that arrived there every hour. During the war Scapa Flow had two ferry connections. One of them was serviced by a former mail steamer, *Sir John Hawkins*, and connected Lyness and Longhope with Scapa Pier. The other one was a roundabout connection – the ship would travel between Lyness, Houton, Stromness, Flotta, St Margaret's Hope and the ports on the islands of Cava and Fara.

At that time HMS *Proserpine*, the base at Lynesse, developed a "foothold" in northern Scotland. The outpost was called *Proserpine-Thurso*. Its personnel were coordinating transport to and from the base with the train movements which, as during the Great War, carried military personnel between the north and areas in the south. It was an incarnation of the famous Jellicoe Express. Connections via Pentland Firth were serviced by two transports: the *Earl of Zetland* would depart from Stromness and carried mainly soldiers and the *St Ninian* (known from the Great War), based at Lyness, transported navy personnel.

In 1943, the number of smaller ships reached its peak, escorts, guard ships and minesweepers. Their base was unofficially named Drifter Pool and was designated HMS *Pleiades*. Most of about 100 small ships (organised in the 71st and 72nd Antisubmarine Drifter Groups) were built to order of the Admiralty, according to a design which after the war was to allow the vessels to be rebuilt as fishing boats. They were designated MFV (Motor Fishing Vessel). However, the commanding officer of the drifters, who had his command station on the *Duncan Castle*, quickly realised that the "real" pre-war drifters (they were often ships used during the Great War) were more effective than the MFVs. That observation was confirmed in the post war period when the civilian fishing industry was not particularly interested in the vessels. Two of the ships ended their careers as the Orkney ferries *Hoy Head* and *Watchful*, as the fishermen deemed then unfit for fishing. After the war Poland received five MFVs (built after the conclusion of hostilities) as part of aid received from the United Nations Relief and Rehabilitation Administration.

Simultaneously, the boom and net barrage system reached its final form. The commanding officer of this defensive element was responsible for 6.51 nautical miles of steel nets and booms. Three of the most important obstacle systems cut through Hoxa Sound, Switha Sound and Hoy Sound. Each of them comprised a boom barrier and two lines of net barriers, complemented by a system of hydrophones and mine barrages controlled remotely from the shore. Additional net lines were installed inside the anchorage to protect the berthed ships. The entire system was serviced by 16 surface ships, 1,100 military personnel and 130 civilian workers, employed mainly in the maintenance workshops. The depot ship for the forces working on the barriers was the *Exmouth*, chartered by the Admiralty. Later she served as a submarine depot ship.

The British command had a serious issue securing ships anchored at Scapa Flow from aerial torpedo attacks. In such a case the nets were not fully effective. The Royal Navy was fully aware of that fact after analysing the after-action reports from the attack against the Italian naval base at Taranto (in many ways similar to the base at Scapa Flow). There were attempts to obscure the anchorage with a smoke screen produced by smoke generators installed on the island of Cava. The result depended on wind conditions and did not guarantee the required effectiveness. Another solution tested was the use of a tarpaulin screen strengthened by steel wires. The 10-metre-high, six-mile-long cover was raised on the water by landing craft. Experiments with the protective screen were aborted when all landing craft were sent to fulfil their duty during the invasion of Normandy.

In 1942, the submarine detection system that had so far utilised passive devices (hydrophones) was reinforced by active devices – hydro-acoustic stations identical to those used on escort ships. Two such sonars were installed in Hoxa Sound. Their task was to identify underwater objects detected earlier by the hydrophones and to get a fix on their course and speed. The passive means were unable to do that as they worked in a binary system – there is a target or there is no target – only roughly estimating the enemy's position according to the signal strength. The devices were mostly ineffective. With strong tidal currents moving huge masses of water of different density, the number of false signals was very high. The other two active sonars installed in 1944 farther south in the waters of the Pentland Firth were constantly damaged by storms.

The heavy cruiser USS Wichita in heavy Orkney seas. (NH, 80-G-21010).

In the middle of World War II, the ships in Scapa Flow were anchored according to the following scheme:
- battleships, battlecruisers, fleet aircraft carriers – south east of the island of Fara,
- escort carriers, cruisers – south of the island of Cava,
- destroyers, frigates – at Gutter Sound,
- mine-sweepers – at Outer Hope,
- tankers – north of the island of Cava,
- ammunition transports – west of the island of Cava,
- supply ships, floating stores – at the eastern part of Ore Bay and at West Weddel Sound,
- boom barrage service ships – at Rysa Sound.

Just as in World War I the British command paid particular attention to matters of rest and recreation of military personnel, and the state of health of the northern garrison. In spite of appearances, those two things were strictly connected with each other. When people from the south arrived at the Orkney Islands, they would very often encounter depression caused by the small amount of daylight during autumn and winter months. Medics, half in jest, half seriously, distinguished a new medical condition and called it *Melancholia Orcadensis*.

Medical services also had to deal with health issues caused by the humid and windy Orkney climate. Despite not being a serious threat to patients' health, these problems were difficult to treat due to limited medical resources. In 1939, the entire medical services of the Lynesse base were contained in two barracks. The situation improved after two hospital ships, the *Varna* and the *Amarapoora*, arrived at Scapa Flow. Later, a military hospital was built at Kirkwall. It treated not only military personnel but also the civilian population of the islands. In 1941, a hospital in Houton was opened and medical installations at Lyness had been developed. In 1943, the *Amarapoora* left the islands and was replaced by another hospital ship, the *Isle of Jersey*.

In order to maintain good psychological condition of soldiers, the men and their units were rotated. The rotation took place within the area subordinate to the OSDef and on the whole British islands. To move troops the OSDef had its own transport ship, the *Earl of Zetland*. She was also used to transport men on leave between Stromness and Scabster.

The Orkney and Shetland garrison also developed an educational service responsible for inspiring and arranging artistic creativity and other forms of intellectual activity. There were amateur music and theatre groups, dancing parties were organised with participation of females from different auxiliary services and from Orkney itself. Among many other projects, the educational service published a newspaper, "The Orkney Blast", and had a radio station which broadcast information and entertainment programs. Concerts and plays with professional artists were often organised and the cinemas were working constantly. The halls were on land (the Garrison Theatre was built at Kirkwall) and aboard ships. These chambers were on auxiliary ships, the *Dunluce Castle* and the *Autocarrier*. As during the previous war, sport was also a very important part of the off-duty activities. Football and other matches were organised, however, the most popular was boxing – mainly because of the gambling prospects.

A surprisingly large number of soldiers – like the sailors twenty years earlier – took on gardening. There were at least two reasons. The first one was very simple, there was a need for fresh vegetables to supplement the food rations, the other one was connected with the activity itself as it provided relaxation.

The *Dunluce Castle* and the *Autocarrier* were also used as floating canteens and service centres, which included hairdressers, shoemakers, laundries, ironing facilities and others. The drifter crews also had a similar ship, the *William Archibald*. A military canteen network was also built on land.

In August 1941, the island garrison was in state of readiness due to a planned visit from the Prime Minister, Churchill. He was on his way, aboard the battleship HMS *Prince of Wales*, to meet the President of the United States, Franklin D. Roosevelt. The ship carrying Churchill departed from Scapa Flow on August 4 and returned after the conference and the prime minister's visit to Iceland on August 18.

The submarines HMS Unbroken and Uther at Scapa Flow, following their return from a successful patrol, October 1943. (WM (A 19983)

The destroyer ORP Burza *at Scapa Flow, date unknown. (IWM, FL 22704).*

In August 1941 and March 1943, the Orkney Islands were again visited by King George VI. During the latter visit, the destroyer HMS *Milne*, carrying the king, was escorted by the ORP *Orkan*. The last wartime visit from the monarch took place between May 10 and May 13, 1945. George VI was accompanied by the King of Norway, Haakon VII, and the King of Greece, George II. It was the only time in the islands' history when three monarchs visited the place simultaneously.

At the beginning of 1944, a slow process of withdrawal of British forces from the Orkney Islands began. The war still raged on, with the enemy controlling Norway only 300 nautical miles from the island, however the real threat level for Scapa Flow decreased significantly. Although transferring several batteries of anti-aircraft searchlights at the beginning of 1943 was a singular event, the decision made in February 1944 to redeploy three heavy anti-aircraft batteries from the Scapa Flow garrison marked the beginning of a constant running-down process.

In June 1944 when the navy scuttled the last wrecks at Burra Sound, the air force command made a decision to withdraw all barrage balloons from the Orkney Islands. They were redeployed to London, that was under constant threat from the V-1 flying bomb attacks. The RAF security regiment was also redeployed to the mainland, right after the barrage balloons. Another unit whose presence on the islands was deemed unnecessary was 70th Anti-Aircraft Artillery Regiment. The number of unmanned anti-aircraft artillery stations would increase month after month.

Anti-submarine net ready to be laid by a special purpose vessel operating in Gutter Sound. (NA, ref. ADM116/5790).

Boom and net barrage depot ship HMS Pomona *in Lyness. 1943. (NA, ref. ADM116/5790)*

HMS Renown *photographed in Orkney, probably in 1927.*

A Queen Elizabeth *class battleship with an R class submarine, 1930s. (A. Jarski's collection)*

HMS Victorious *during her operations with the Home Fleet.* HMS Rodney *or the* Nelson *can be seen in the background.*

US warships at Scapa Flow. The heavy cruiser Wichita *can be seen in the foreground, with the aircraft carrier USS* Wasp *in the background. (NH, 97884)*

The submarine HMS Ultimatum *passing behind the stern of the armed drifter* Stella Pegasi *during manoeuvres in June 1943. (IWM, A 17174)*

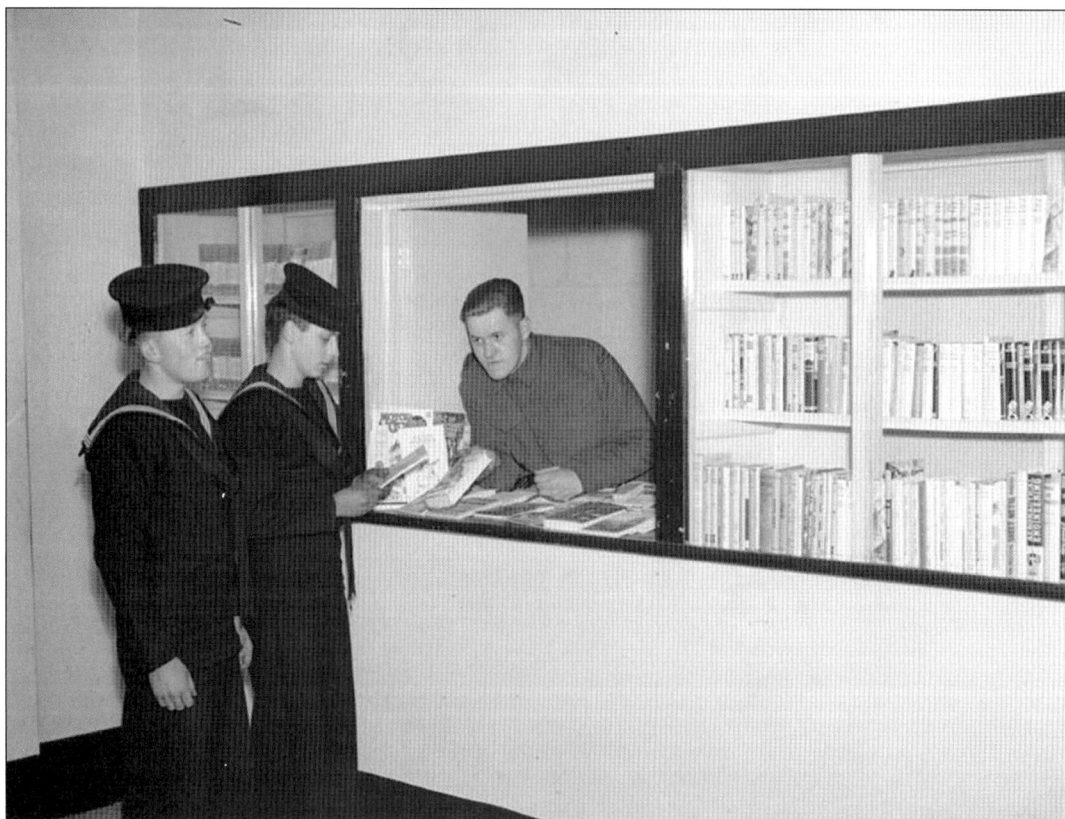

Beginning of June 1944. The light cruiser Belfast departing Scapa Flow. She was the flagship of Bombardment Force E, supporting troops landing at Gold and Juno beaches.

An apparently staged photo of British seamen returning books at Lyness library (IWM, A 24850).

The battleship USS Washington on her way to Great Britain, April 22, 1942. (NH, 80-G-21029)

Stern of the destroyer ORP Błyskawica, damaged in a collision with the British destroyer HMS Musketeer. *The accident happened at Scapa Flow in late February 1944. (IWM, A 22167)*

Scharnhorst *survivors at Scapa Flow, January 2, 1944.*

U-boats against Scapa Flow
– the final attempt

The routine of everyday service could not make one forget that the war was still raging on and the threat was lurking not only in the air but also in the waters surrounding Orkney.

In November 1944, the German submarine command organised an operation in waters around the Orkney Islands to intercept and destroy British forces (including aircraft carriers) operating in the North Atlantic. The operation was based on the false assumption that the enemy forces operated from the Scapa Flow base. The following submarines were deployed for the operation:

- *U-1020*, Type VIIC/41,
- *U-739*, Type VIIC,
- *U-312*, Type VIIC,
- *U-737*, Type VIIC,
- *U-775*, Type VIIC,
- *U-315*, Type VIIC,
- *U-278*, Type VIIC,
- *U-297*, Type VIIC/41.

The heavy cruiser USS Tuscaloosa *at anchor in Scapa Flow, April 1942. (NH, 80-G-12018)*

A group of destroyers led by the HMS Fury *arrives at Scapa Flow, 1942. (IWM, A 10296)*

The submarines were deployed west of the Orkney Islands with the task of patrolling the approaches to Hoy Sound. Despite the German assumption that the British did not operate in large groups on these waters, they did carry out extensive search and destroy operations against submarines, with use of the air force and search and destroy naval groups.

On December 6 a group of British ships (19th Escort Group) composed of the destroyer HMS *Hesperus* (H 57, ex-*Hearty*, ex-Brazilian *Juruena*, Havant class), the escort destroyer HMS *Bullen* (ex-US DE 78 Buckley class), frigates HMS *Loch Insh* (K 433, Loch class) and *Goodall* (K 479, Captain class) was conducting search operations around the shores of northern Scotland, manoeuvring around Cape Wrath.

At about 10.00 hours, the German submarine *U-775*, that had earlier detected the Allied escorts, took position for an attack and fired two torpedoes at HMS *Bullen*. One of them hit amidships and exploded between the boiler room and the engine room, which broke the destroyer's hull in half. Being unaware of the reason for the explosion (lack of a torpedo wake suggests that *U-775* fired an electric torpedo, not a gas-steam propelled one) and facing the possibility of the *Bullen* being destroyed by a mine,

The Canadian "four-piper" St. Croix (ex-USS McCook*) at the approaches during her transit from Orkney to Iceland, mid 1941. (U.S. Naval History and Heritage Command, NH 70079).*

81

one of the British ships (the *Goodall*) lowered a lifeboat and began rescue operation. Simultaneously, the *Hesperus* and *Loch Insh* were searching the waters with their sonar. The former made contact with a submarine, made a turn and headed full ahead towards the detected enemy. Unfortunately, a wave created by the destroyer overturned the boat from the *Goodall* which resulted in drowning of several survivors and crew members of the lifeboat.

During the next 14 hours, the three British escorts searched for the submarine, periodically losing and making sonar contact. A dozen or so depth charges were dropped, however, no debris appeared on the surface to indicate a successful attack. Finally, *U-775* managed to escape and returned to her base in Norway. The submarine survived until the end of the war and was then sunk during "Operation Deadlight" on December 8, 1945

Three hours after HMS *Bullen* had been torpedoed, a Short Sunderland Mk.III of 210 Squadron of 15 Group Coastal Command Group left the Castle Archdale base (at Lough Erne) in Northern Ireland. Initially, it conducted a routine patrol mission north of the Scottish coast. At 10.40 the radio operator received (via the coastal command station) a signal from the ships searching for a submarine. The aircraft changed its course and headed towards the ships to begin cooperation.

The Sunderland reached its new patrol area at 10.53. The plane's crew noticed the remains of HMS *Bullen* floating on the surface. The aircraft made a circle over the life boats and headed north-east. After several hours of patrolling, at 16.43, the flying boat saw a small cloud of white smoke. The pilot

The aircraft carrier USS Ranger *with the British cruiser HMS* Belfast *in action against German shipping in Norway, October 1943. (IWM, A 19598)*

The destroyer ORP Garland *probably at the approaches to Scapa Flow, April 7, 1945. (IWM, FL 8921).*

decreased altitude to 70 metres. At a distance of one mile the crew saw a wake on the surface. It was caused by the snorkel of a submerged submarine. The submarine's speed was estimated at 10-12 knots, on a north-east course. The aircraft attacked the enemy but the depth charge release system failed. The Sunderland made a circle and repeated the attack. This time, with no complications, six depth charges hit their mark.

The submarine stood no chance. She was completely destroyed within several seconds. The aircraft remained in the area for about 20 minutes. A large oil spill appeared on the surface. The plane's crew had no doubt, they had sunk the submarine. The Sunderland returned to base at 21.23 after a 14 hour and 13 minute mission.

The naval air force command had a different opinion concerning the effects of the flying boat's mission. The Sunderland's attack was not confirmed as a kill, not even a U-boat damaged, but only as an "attack against a submarine". The first post-war combat records stated that U-297, having torpedoed HMS Bullen, was sunk by the Loch Insh and the Goodall. Only after comparing the German and British documents was it possible to correct the mistake. It turned out that the British escort had fallen victim to U-775, and U-297 (with a "missing" status in the German documents) had been sunk by the aircraft. It also explained why the commanding officer of U-297 was completely surprised by the aerial attack. He was not aware of the fact that, after sinking the destroyer, his area of operations became active with the enemy's anti-submarine forces. Additionally, the Sunderland detected the submarine visually and not with radar. The U-boat was fitted with devices that would have warned her commander of being scanned by radar.

The irony of the situation is that the aircraft's crew did not have an opportunity to celebrate their late success. On March 14, 1945, the Sunderland manned by the crew that had sunk U-297 crashed in the hills near Killybegs.

"Operation Diana" did not bring the German command the results they had anticipated. Of eight submarines deployed west of the Orkney Islands, only one succeeded – she sank the escort destroyer. It came at the cost of one U-boat lost.

The wreckage of U-297 was not discovered until 2000. Although the submarine's resting place had been marked on fishing maps as a point where fishing boats would tear their nets, the fact was not connected to a sunk submarine. On March 4, two divers from Stromness discovered the wreckage and identified it as a German Type VII submarine. Further diving and search operations made it possible to confirm the identity of the U-boat. U-297 rests at a depth of 86 metres with about 30° list to starboard. Serious damage is visible at the conning tower and on the deck in front of the conning tower, indicating the place where a depth charge sealed the submarine's fate.

Arthur Askey and Jack Hylton as guest artists at New Home Fleet Theatre. 18 July 1943, Scapa Flow. A number of well known performers including Arthur Askey, Jack Hylton, "Georgina" and June Marlow, were guest artists at the New Home Fleet Theatre opened by Admiral Sir Bruce Fraser, C-in-c Home Fleet. The New Theatre, which seated 1,236 officers and men, was built by the Royal Marine Engineers. (IWM A 18140)

The end of the war and the post-war decline

The biggest decrease of British forces in the Orkney Islands took place in January 1945. Due to the fact that major operations had moved south and Scapa Flow was less and less used by large task forces of the fleet, a decision was made to leave only 24 heavy gun emplacements around Lyness. The remaining guns, along with anti-aircraft searchlights and other equipment, left the island.

The coastal batteries had undergone a similar process earlier. When the "Churchill barriers" cut through the eastern straits, the continued presence of the batteries was not necessary. On November 15, 1943, a battery of 76 mm guns was withdrawn. The turrets with twin 57 mm guns were dismounted from their position at Holm and were to be placed at South Walls. Some publications claim that never came to be. An identical turret dismounted from its position on the island of Burray was moved to Graemsay. The dismissed crews of the coastal batteries were transferred to the infantry, which suffered from a permanent shortage of men, or to field artillery regiments.

The battleship USS Washington *at Scapa Flow, October 1942. The photo was taken from the deck of the aircraft carrier USS* Wasp. *(U.S. Navy National Museum of Naval Aviation photo No. 1967.038.0310).*

The news of a ceasefire in Europe reached the island on Monday, May 7, 1945. However, many Orkney families were not relieved as their loved ones were still fighting on the other side of the world in Asia, where no end of hostilities was in sight. The 226th Heavy Anti-aircraft Battery of the 101st Anti-aircraft Artillery Regiment was still involved in the campaign in Burma. That is why May saw little celebration on the island, whereas the real festivities began after the surrender of Japan.

The end of the war in Europe did not mean the end of anxiety for their relatives but it increased the process of demilitarisation of Scapa Flow. The process was faster than after World War I, when the Orkney anchorage became a place of internment for the German fleet. There was also another difference. Two decades earlier the coastal guns were just scrapped and this time they were dismounted from their positions, carefully maintained and prepared for long-term storage in the navy arsenal.

Between 1945 and 1946 mine-sweeping operations were extremely limited in comparison to those after World War I. After the end of hostilities only 10 minesweepers took part in mine searching operations. The ships checked the waters around Orkney and a large area of the North Sea. There were no Americans who, after the Great War, had a huge impact on the economy of the islands. Although the cruiser USS *Little Rock* and two destroyers stayed in Scapa Flow in July 1946, it did not compare to the earlier "invasion" of the American minesweeper crews.

At that time the history of Orkney was intertwined with Polish history. The barrack compounds left by the British troops became a place for settlement of the Polish army troops who were not needed by their Anglo-Saxon allies any more. 25th Infantry Battalion was placed in the Tornisson Camp at Stenness and in the Hillside Camp on South Ronaldsay. The newly formed motorised company was placed in the Brig of Waithe Camp. These units, later converted to elements of the Polish Resettlement Corps, remained on the islands for the next few months. The Poles left the island sailing south aboard the *St Ninian*, an old ship of merit for Orkney, that had been especially chartered for them.

Demilitarisation of Orkney heavily impacted the local labour market. The inhabitants tried to comfort themselves with the thought that in the future Scapa Flow would become a NATO base for three fleets, British, American and Canadian. However, that turned out to be wishful thinking. In 1951 the battleship HMS *Vanguard*, the aircraft carriers HMS *Indomitable* and HMS *Indefatigable* along with numerous escort ships, arrived at the anchorage but it had limited influence on the islanders' lives.

In June 1956, the Admiralty announced that, due to a limited defence budget, the Lyness base was to become nothing more than a fuel station. Of 125 civilian personnel only 25 people kept their jobs. It was a real disaster for the inhabitants of Hoy and South Walls who had been making their living by working around the navy installations. However, that did not mean the reductions were over. Due to further cuts in the defence budget, the Royal Navy was forced to leave the Orkney Islands. On March 29, 1957, the White Ensign was lowered from the flagpole, marking the navy's final withdrawal from the penultimate islands.

The battleship
USS Washington.
(NH, 19-N-24147)

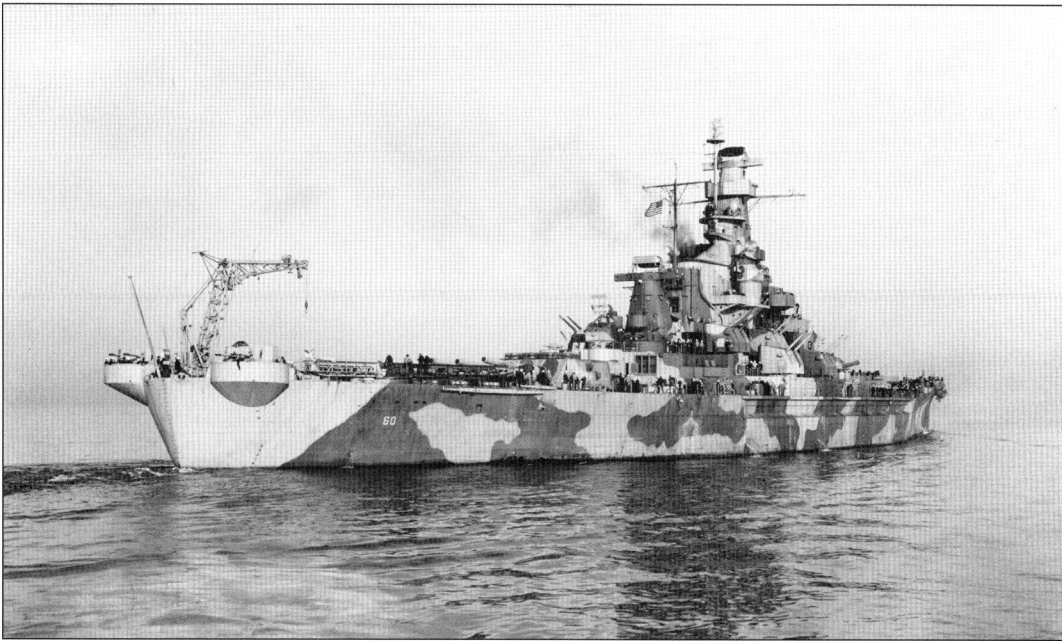

The battleship
USS Alabama, *1943.*
(NH 48136)

Military cemetery on Hoy,
where the sailors and soldiers
fallen during both world
wars found their resting
place. (K. Kubiak)

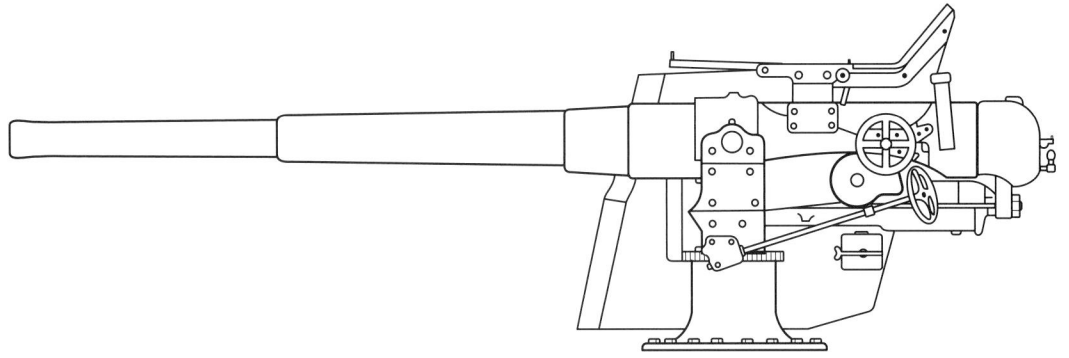

4.7" Quick Firer (WW 1).

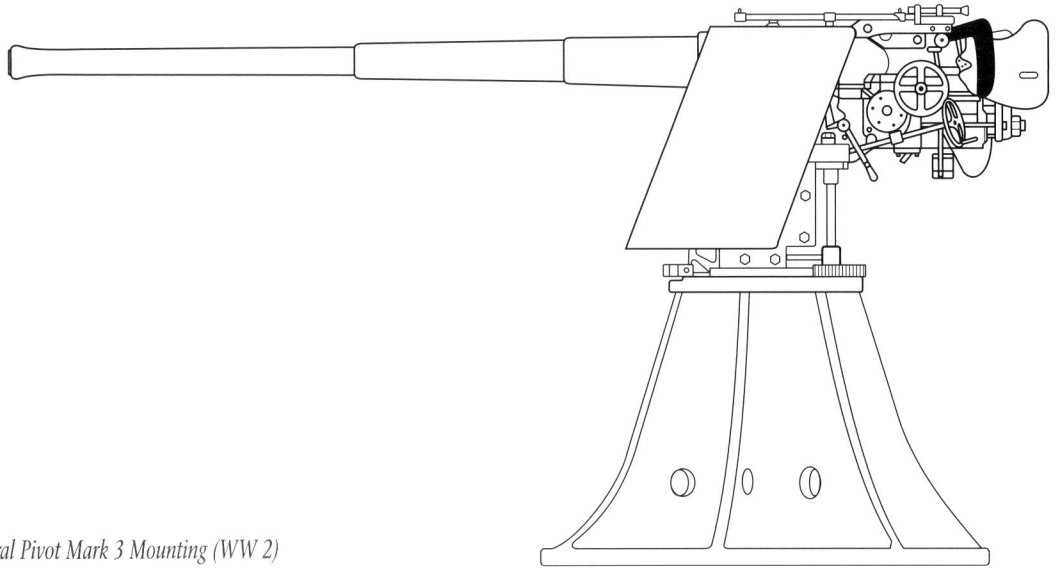

4.7" Quick Firer Mark 4 on Central Pivot Mark 3 Mounting (WW 2)

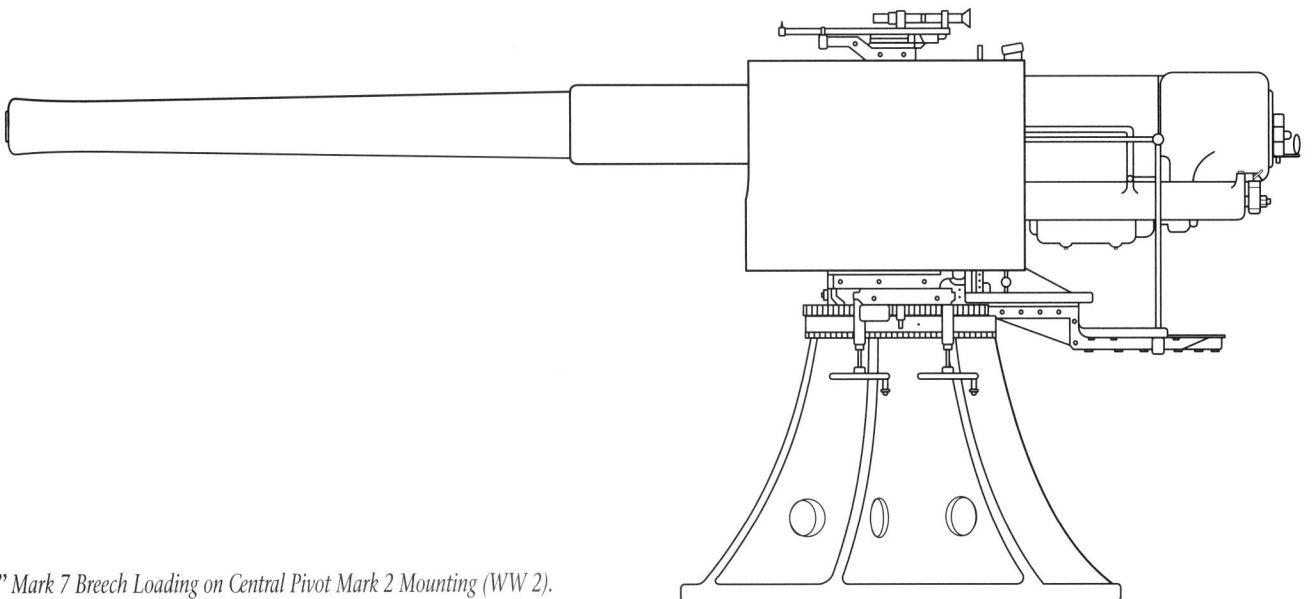

6" Mark 7 Breech Loading on Central Pivot Mark 2 Mounting (WW 2).

Drawings Robert Panek

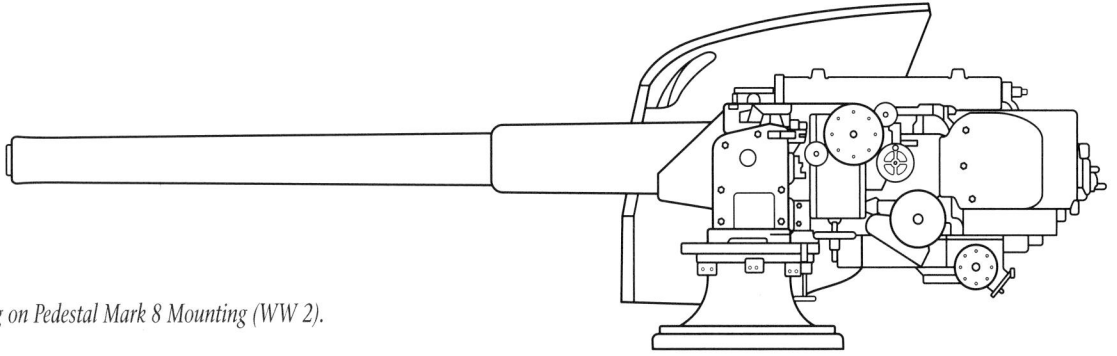

6" Mark 7 Breech Loading on Pedestal Mark 8 Mounting (WW 2).

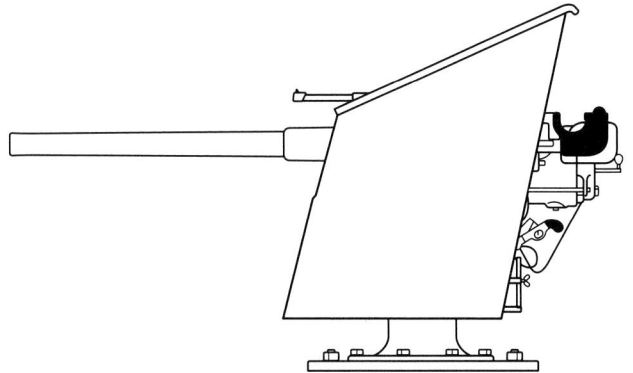

12 Pounder Quick Firer Mark 1 (WW 2).

Twin 6 Pounder Quick Firer Mark 1 (WW 2).

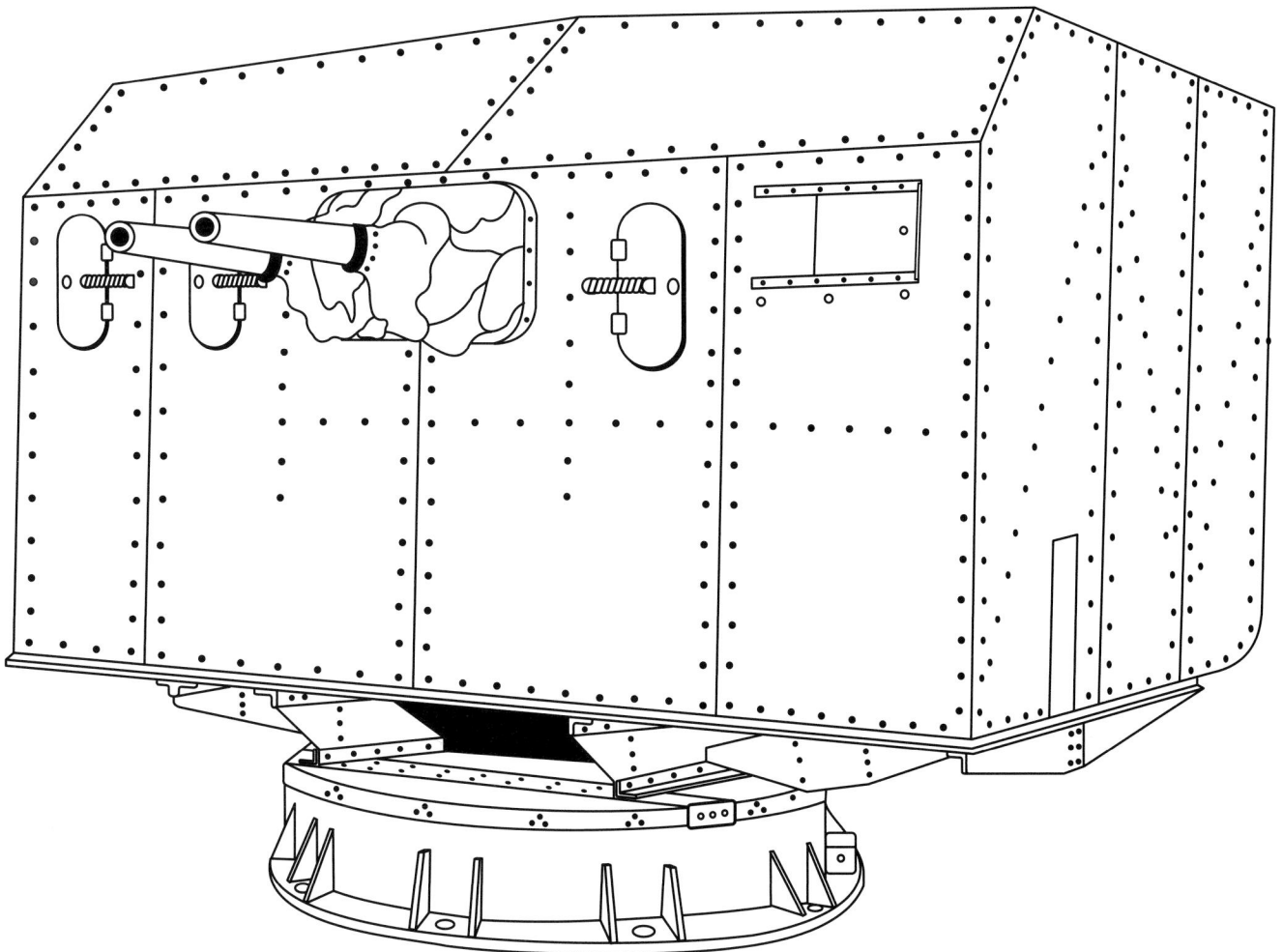

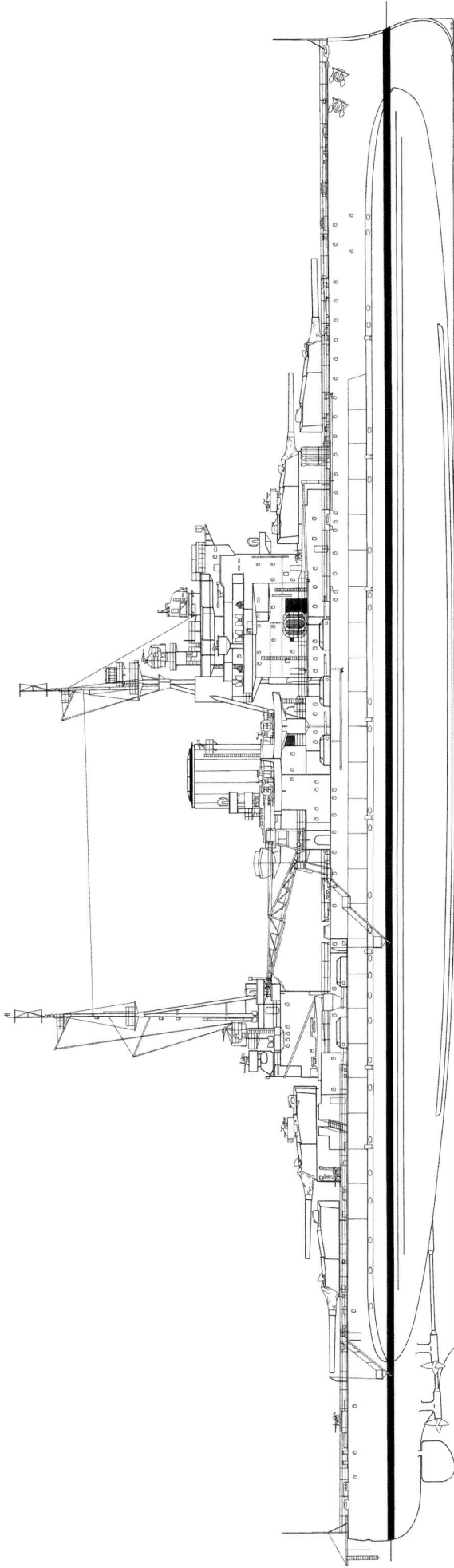

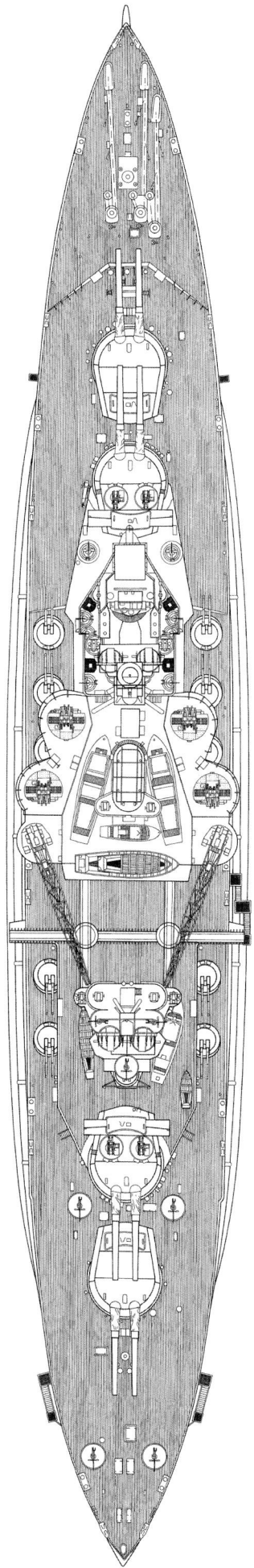

HMS Queen Elizabeth.

Drawings Witold Koszela

90

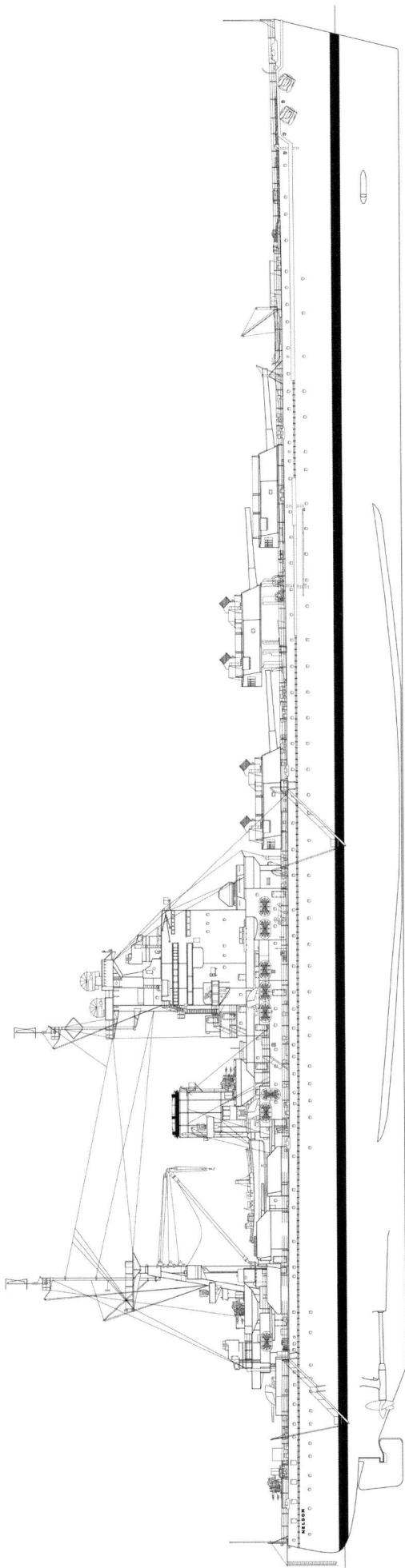

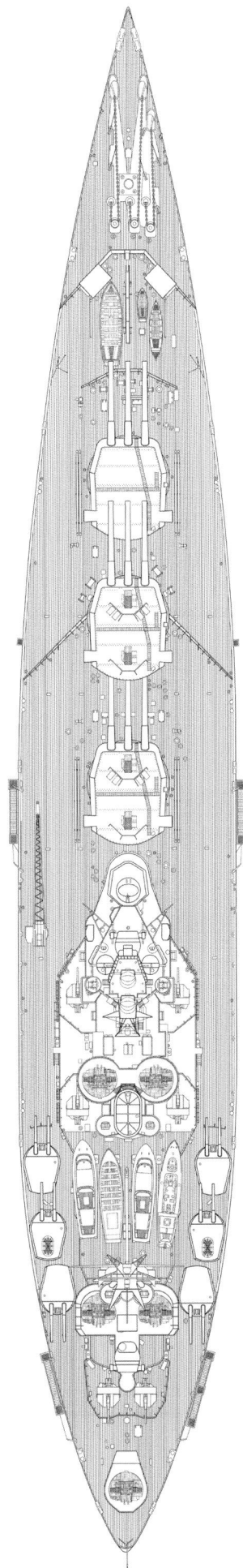

Drawings Witold Koszela

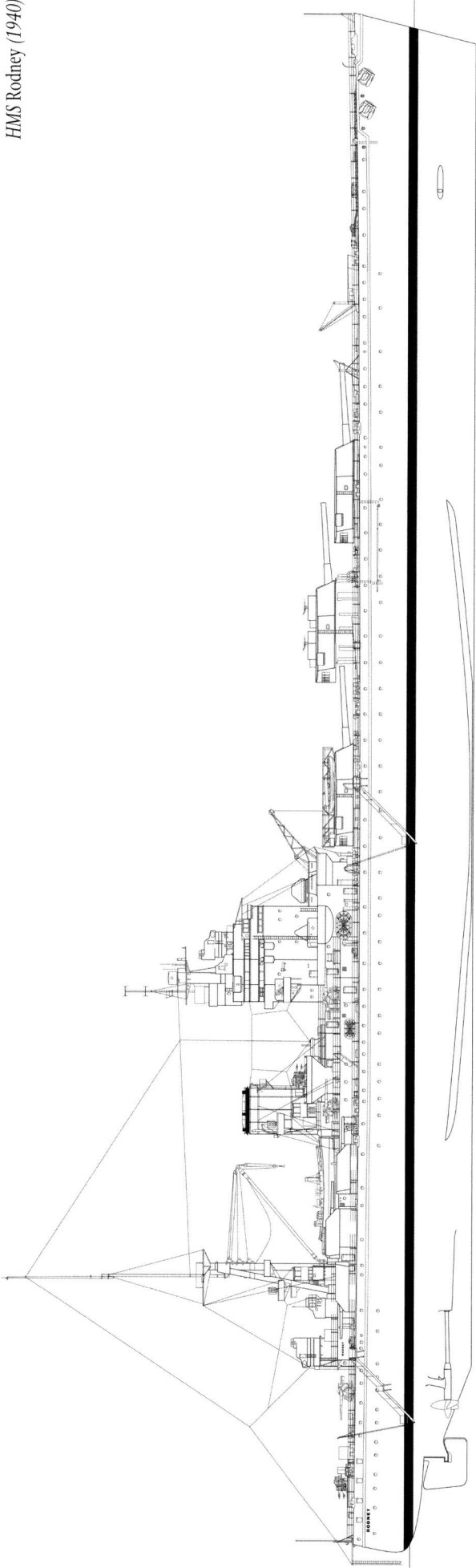

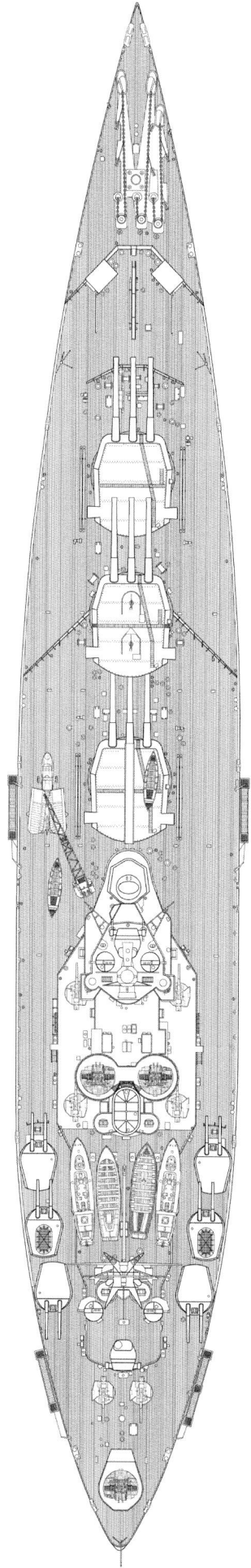

Drawings Witold Koszela

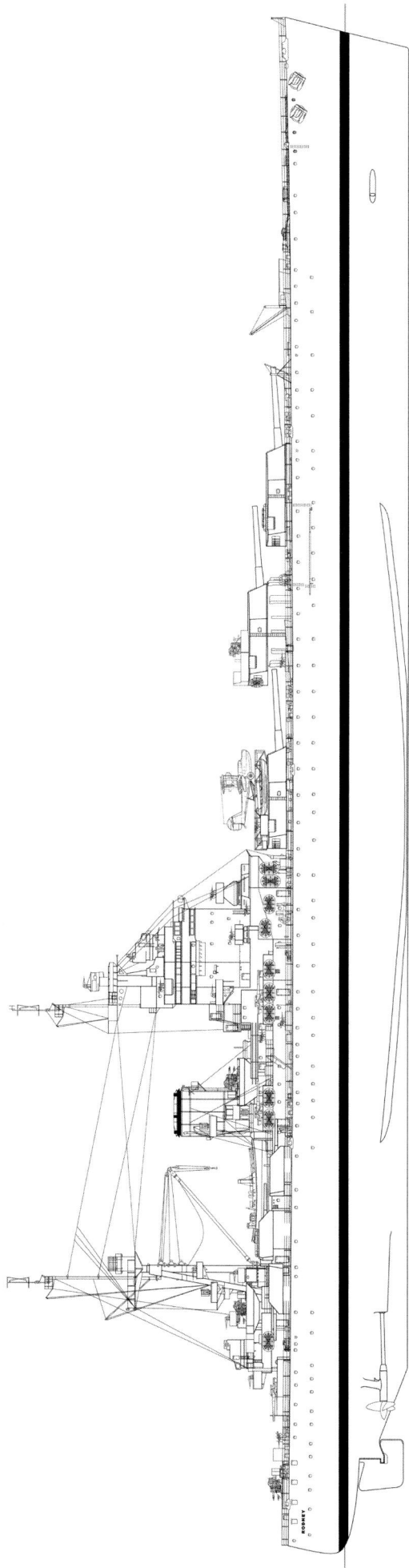

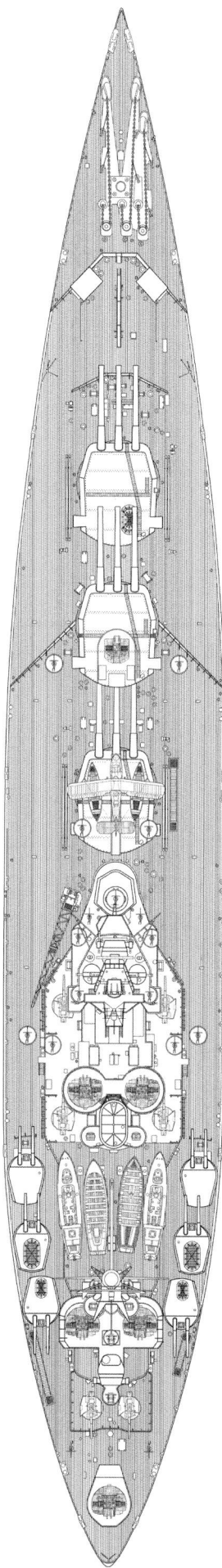

HMS Rodney (1944).

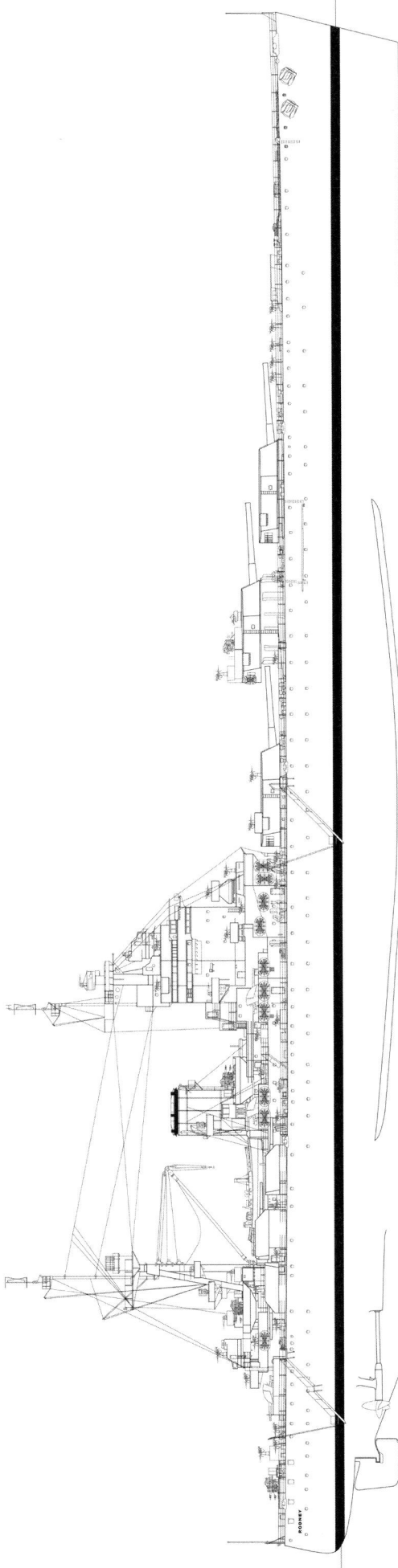

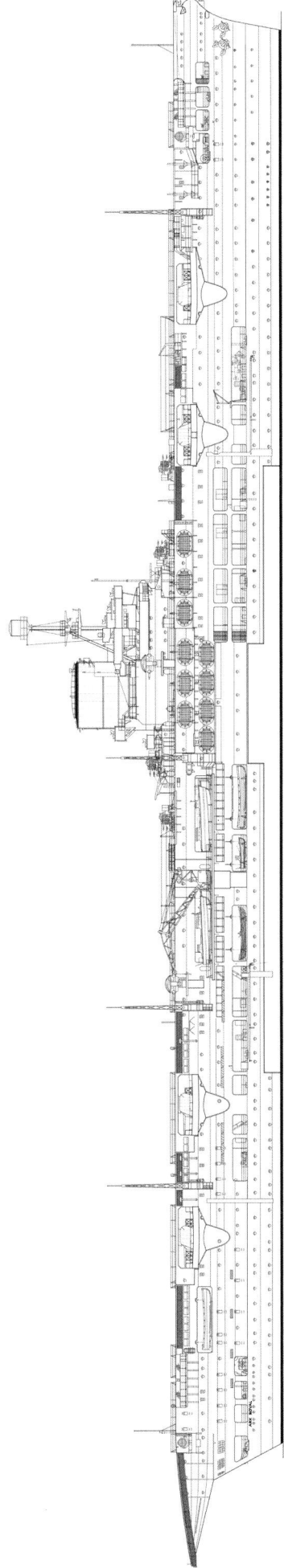

HMS Ark Royal.

Drawings Witold Koszela

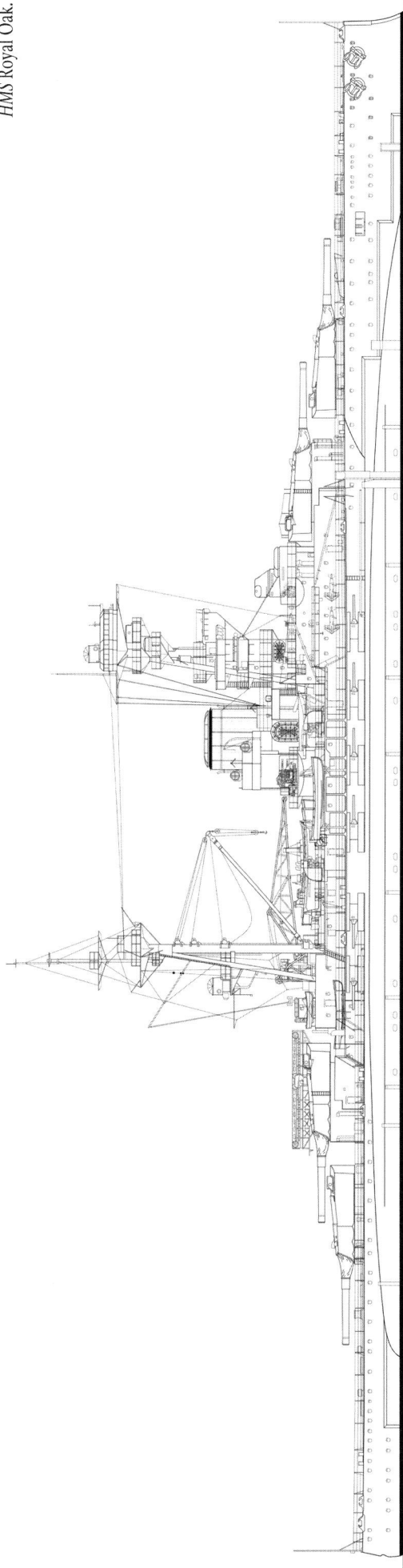

HMS Royal Oak.

Drawings Witold Koszela

Ship Name Index